WISDOM
WINS!

FINDING THE PATH OF GODLY WISDOM FOR YOUR LIFE

STEPHEN MATTHEW

RIVER
PUBLISHING

River Publishing & Media Ltd
Barham Court
Teston
Maidstone
Kent
ME18 5BZ
United Kingdom

info@river-publishing.co.uk

ISBN 978-1-908393-51-7
Cover design by www.spiffingcovers.com
Printed in the United Kingdom by Bell and Bain Ltd, Glasgow

Find out more about the author by visiting:
www.stephenmatthew.com
Twitter: @StephenMatthew_
Facebook: pastorStephenMatthew

Contents

What People Are Saying About
Wisdom Wins!

"The Bible says 'Wisdom is supreme' and in this excellent book Stephen unlocks some of the key ways into its supremacy. It is practical and thoroughly biblical, a 'must read' for anyone who is serious about living in a manner that pleases God and desires to fulfill their destiny."

John Partington
National Leader of Assemblies of God GB

"I've had the privilege of knowing and working with Stephen for over 30 years and have benefitted from his calm, measured wisdom more times than I can count. So, I can't recommend this book enough. It is well-written, unpacking big themes in his characteristically clear style, and best of all, is very practical. Read it and tell others to read it, because here is wisdom for life in a world so often devoid of it."

Paul Scanlon
Founding Pastor of Life Church, Bradford

"Daniel is described as being wise *'in both books and in life'* (1:17 The Message). That winning combination made him outstanding.
* Some people are clever with books not life
* Some are good with life not books
My friend Stephen has the Daniel kind of wisdom in spades and passes it on accessibly in this practical and insightful book to make us wise in life."

Anthony Delaney
Ivy Church Network
& New Thing Europe

"A book has great value when it is birthed out of the heart and experience of its writer. *Wisdom Wins!* is such a book. Stephen's passion to see strong, strategic churches built has drilled down to one word, 'wisdom'. He offers seven pillars that are essential if we are to build thriving lives and churches. Only a wisely built life and church community will stand when the winds and waves of change and pressure challenge it."

Stuart Bell
Senior Pastor of Alive Church
& Leader of the Ground Level Network

"I've known Stephen for many years and have no hesitation in recommending this wonderfully written book and the wisdom it contains. It flows from a father's heart and his lifelong commitment to helping people find the wisdom God wants them to walk in. For pastors, it will help you to understand your people better. And for the rest of us … who does not need more wisdom? I believe you will 'win', your friends and family will 'win', and the Kindgom of God will be the ultimate winner if you will read and live this book."

John Kirkby
Founder of CAP – Christians Against Poverty

"Much can be said about wisdom. On one hand it can be biblical, theoretical and logical, but on the other it has to be exemplified, demonstrated and lived out. These two come together in this great book. I've known Stephen for many years and he lives this book. He writes well and lives what he writes. Highly recommended!"

Dr Scott Wilson
President Eurolead.net

"Such a good book and much needed! In it you will discover that true wisdom is only found in a relationship with the person of

Wisdom – Jesus. Stephen skilfully unpacks how to do this by building your life around seven pillars of wisdom that will not only shape your life and character, but will also impact those you do life with."

Clive Urquhart
Senior Pastor, Kingdom Faith Church, UK

"I would recommend this book to anyone who is seriously pursuing wisdom. Stephen shares some insightful ways of gaining wisdom for life and explains its true nature and source. It is clearly the fruit of his personal 'wisdom journey' and provides the reader with a practical and comprehensive resource of how to both get wisdom and use it."

David Belfield
Senior Pastor, Today's Community Church, Wigan

"This book is a great leadership tool. Following the quality of his previous titles, it is no surprise that Stephen once again successfully connects the spiritual and the practical in his own unique style. He takes the potentially complicated subject of wisdom and makes it accessible to us all. It is not only worth a read, it demands to be lived."

Pawel Godawa
Senior Pastor, Water of Life Christian Centre, Poland

"*Wisdom Wins!* is a simple but great book. Stephen has taken what to many is a slightly mystical subject, just out of their reach, and put it firmly within their grasp. The book really is a 'must read' for every leader and for those wanting to grow in wisdom. It is practical, Christ-centered and an easy read. I wholeheartedly commend it and will be using it within our church context."

Steve Uppal
Senior Leader, All Nations Christian Centre, Wolverhampton

Introduction:
"A bit of wisdom"

A bit of wisdom

It happened again this week. In fact, it has happened most weeks of my ministry life. Someone from the congregation approached me and asked me what, on the face of it, is a simple question: *"Steve, can you just give me a bit of wisdom about how to handle my situation..."*

If only it was that simple! It rarely is.

I have been a church Pastor for well over 30 years. And as any church leader will tell you, there is a certain expectation on those of us called into Christian ministry to be wise. Of course, an appropriate humility prevents any of us claiming to be the fount of all wisdom. But we do believe we serve a God who is. So we frequently find ourselves sandwiched between an all-knowing God who is the source of wisdom and his people who are desperately seeking it.

When people ask their pastor or spiritual leaders that simple question, they are not necessarily asking them 'what to do' but simply for the benefit of their experience in what may be a complex situation. They know God has the answer and they believe the Bible contains principles that will help them navigate the issue. They have probably been racking their brain considering all the options and praying hard for guidance. What they just need now is a 'bit of wisdom' to encourage them along the way.

Dealing with the wonderful people God entrusted to my pastoral care over the years, coupled with my own pursuit of wisdom for living, have resulted in me writing this book. I have come to the conclusion that the request for 'a bit of wisdom' is one of the most frequently asked questions by every Christian, probably most days of their life! But I also believe that the last thing they need is a book of stock answers. We are a people of grace and relationship, not a people of law and dictatorship. So this is not a book of simplistic answers, but one that will point you resolutely along the way of wisdom, helping you to walk in a close relationship with God and draw on the wisdom of his grace every step of the way.

My prayer is that as we explore this wonderful theme together, you will soon understand that *Wisdom Wins!* It wins the argument, the war, the battle and ultimately the prize. So, it becomes of paramount importance to *'Get Wisdom'* (Proverbs 4:7).

Part 1:
The Way of Wisdom

"Listen, my son, accept what I say,
and the years of your life will be many.
I instruct you in the way of wisdom
and lead you along straight paths."
(Proverbs 4:10-11)

Chapter 1
It's Complicated

Thanks for picking this book up. I really do believe it will help you. But first can I ask why you did so?

I thought so. And I have to agree: it's complicated!

You are a complicated person. The people you do life with are complicated too. Then there is the big wide world we live in, the complexity of which never ceases to amaze me.

Life is so complicated that we have developed experts in every field of study imaginable. You name it and there will be an 'ology' relating to it. I'm interested in God, so theology is my thing. But then, I love the dynamics of building church in unique contexts, so ecclesiology is close to my heart too. When I climb the hills I draw on my interest in geology and always have to check the climatology before we set off!

Every aspect of life has enough challenge and complexity within it to make us seek the wisdom to do it better or more successfully. So it's little wonder everyone is looking for that "bit of wisdom" they need for their current situation.

The problem with all this is that it implies the wisdom we seek is pure information, a "bolt on" we can acquire. But that is not the case. Wisdom consists of far more than a collection of "bits of wisdom" such as I mentioned in my introduction. True wisdom is something we seek, find, embrace, imbibe and which becomes an essential part of us. Wisdom eventually characterises us. And for that reason, *Wisdom Wins!*

So there is hope, as we shall see.

Winning

Before we get to that, something else strikes me: maybe it was the word "wins" in the book title that made you pick it up, rather than the word "wisdom"? Maybe your issue is that you feel like a loser and want to become a winner in life? If so, this book will help you too. But you will first have to agree with my definition of being a winner. That's because the wisdom we are about to explore ensures a certain kind of "win".

If by winning you mean knocking the competition out of the ring, we are not on the same page yet. If to you winning means winning the argument or the battle, being top of the class, or the first to break the tape, you are still not clear. The wisdom we are about to explore will equip you for one very particular kind of win. That win is personal to you and involves no competition from other people, because it is to do with winning the race you are in against yourself.

Forget competing with other people, just focus on yourself as you read this book. It will equip you with wisdom to be the best "you" you can be. The aim is that you acquire the wisdom needed to release all your inherent potential and become a winner in life. It is about you winning the race against you; beating your past failures, bad habits and social conditioning and becoming the person God destined you to be.

On that basis, we can all win. We just need to discover a wisdom that will help us run our course and reach the finish line successfully. That wisdom will help us navigate life in a happy and fulfilling way, by facilitating the expression of our inherent personality, gifts and abilities, while also helping us make great choices about where to apply them. It will truly make us winners in life.

All this, and more, is why people are looking for wisdom. They crave the skill and wisdom to navigate their complicated daily lives successfully.

But there is hope. Just picking this book up has taken you a step nearer to the wisdom you know you need but have not yet found. And my aim is to take you on a journey of discovery. It will involve understanding what wisdom actually is, how it can be found and most importantly, how it can be applied very practically. You are going to discover that *Wisdom Wins!* And that wisdom can be yours.

Chapter 2
What is Wisdom?

I couldn't help smiling to myself when I first looked up the dictionary definition of wisdom. The prestigious Oxford English Dictionary describes wisdom as *"being wise"* – not that helpful really! And its American counterpart, Websters, says much the same: *"The quality of being wise"*. Maybe from that I should have realised, wisdom is far too profound a thing to be condensed into a few small words of definition!

To be fair, those excellent volumes do go on to explain wisdom a little more, including phrases like *"soundness of judgement in matters of life and conduct"* and one phrase I particularly like: *"The faculty of making the best use of knowledge, experience and understanding"*.

This phrase gets to the root of it. Wisdom is not about knowledge, experience or understanding. It is all about what we do with those things. It is all about the *application*.

The application
Who do you consider to be wise? Stop and think about it for a minute. I would guess that on your list of wise friends are people who you think know a lot. Maybe they are highly qualified

or just good at quizzes. But however their vast knowledge is expressed, you are convinced they could win Mastermind! No doubt your list also contains people who have seen quite a bit of life; people who have been through some ups and downs and been shaped by them. My list certainly had people like that on it. Some have great knowledge, others great experience.

But we have to acknowledge that their knowledge or experience alone is not why they are on our list of wise friends. They are on it because of how they have since applied that knowledge and experience in life. Think of it this way:

Knowledge is about education and learning
Wisdom is about the application of that learning

Knowledge focuses on input
Wisdom focuses on output

Knowledge is about the accumulation of information and facts
Wisdom is more to do with conduct, judgement and making good choices

Knowledge will help you pass an exam
Wisdom will help you build a good marriage, business, church or nation

Experience teaches you how life works
Wisdom ensures you make life work for yourself and those you love

Experience is subjective, it focuses on personal pain or pleasure
Wisdom is objective, it applies experience for the greater good of others

A life that simply accumulates knowledge treats life like a game of Trivial Pursuit, the well-known general knowledge game. Whereas, in reality, life is a game of Chess. It involves knowledge, but more crucially, wise moves, strategy, cunning and foresight.

The complex world we live in as Christians today, simply cannot be managed or lived to the full by following a series of formulas. Life is not "painting by numbers", it is a blank canvas and the choice of possible colours and styles is overwhelming. So whether we end up with a life that looks like a masterpiece or a mess, is all about the skilful application of all we know and experience.

Jesus said, "*Wisdom is proved right by her actions*" (Matthew 11:19). Ultimately, wisdom is seen in the good decisions we make.

I think wisdom has something to do with the quality of our soul, our inner being. Wisdom proceeds from there, from deep within us. It is an ever-deepening reservoir of accumulated knowledge, experiences, observations, conversations and character development that combine to help us make sound choices and good judgements. As we draw deeply on that reservoir, we choose wisely.

The grey

It doesn't take too long for most people to realise that life is not black and white. We would like it to be, but it isn't. Life is not clear cut, tidy, neat and filled with absolutes. Of course there are some, and we should be thankful for them because they provide very clear boundaries and guidelines for successful living. However, if we are honest, most of life is grey.

The "grey" comes from the give and take required to navigate human relationships, our need to respect other people's views and our frequent inability to prove that a position we take is actually the absolute truth. So we make a decision hoping it is the best one in the circumstances. We delve deeply into our reservoir of accumulated knowledge, experience and observations about life, apply that into the situation before us, and make our choice. Was it a wise decision? Well, as Jesus said, *"Wisdom is proved right by her actions"*, so time will tell.

I believe that the wise make good decisions in the grey areas of life. They make the best decisions where it is not necessarily clear cut or where intangible and unquantifiable forces are at work – like people's feelings, reactions, attitudes and perceptions.

We have raised four children of our own and now have the joy of helping them raise our wonderful grandchildren. Raising children is an imprecise skill to say the least! Every child is different and every parent brings a unique life-journey and set of experiences to their parenting role. Parenting books abound to help us and, of course, the Bible gives us some helpful principles to apply too. Yet faced with the daily decisions involved in raising a child, we frequently feel devoid of the practical wisdom needed to make a strong, correct choice.

I mean things like, how do you decide how much TV they should watch? Sounds easy, but you try getting that right when they want to watch their favourite show endlessly, their friends talk incessantly about that particular show, and to be cool they must be up to date with the storyline. Yet you think its excessive, have some doubts about the ethical content of the show and wonder if it is actually getting in the way of their homework from school. So you talk it over with other parents, only to discover that some have banned the show altogether in their house. But you know their children have watched it at yours. Oops! Then others actually watch the show with their kids, buy them the sticker book and magazine associated with it and see it as a great family bonding opportunity. Hmmm.

You ponder, what does the Bible say? What would my parents have done? What would my church's position on this be? Is the show actually damaging my child or am I damaging my child if I ban them from watching it? Aaargh! If only life were simple. I just need a bit of wisdom… Welcome to the grey world of parenting.

Here's another. Little Jimmy reaches an age you consider appropriate for him to be receiving pocket money. The questions simply become, how much does he get and are there any conditions attached to it? Is it just given irrespective of how he has behaved that week? Does he do household chores for it, to teach him a work ethic? One of Jimmy's friends, you soon discover, gets three times what you give him, whereas another friend doesn't get any at all. So are you being generous or stingy? And what should it be spent on? Is it his to do what he wants with or do you require him to put some of it into the church offering to teach Jimmy a giving ethic? Do you suggest he saves some each week? Or is it just for blowing on his weekly sugar fix? And so we could go on.

Some parents would just ban TV and pocket money altogether, others would lavish both on their children as expressions of love towards them. But that "love" can sometimes be to compensate for other inadequacies in their parenting, like not spending enough time with their children; just as the ban could be rooted in unhealthy prejudices and perceptions gathered from their own dysfunctional upbringing.

Two simple issues on the face of it, but more complex once you get into them. What seemed black and white at first glance turned out to be rather grey! That is life. And every day you are making choices about a myriad of "simple" things like these, where your limited knowledge and experience have to be applied with wisdom for the sake of yourself and others.

The good news is that wisdom is available. It is possible

to navigate life successfully in spite of its greyness. You can accumulate sufficient knowledge, experience and a set of guiding principles to wisely apply into every situation you face. I am not talking here about being absolutely right in all and every situation, because there is often no actual right or wrong position to adopt. It is rather about finding the path that leads you into peace, fulfilment and a genuine sense that the decision you made was the wisest in the circumstances and that God is smiling on it.

Finding that path is the subject of the remainder of this book. Returning to the definitions of wisdom we opened this chapter with, my aim is to help you become a person who better exercises *"soundness of judgement in matters of life and conduct"* and one who definitely has *"The faculty of making the best use of knowledge, experience and understanding."*

Chapter 3
Finding It

So, where can we find the elusive "Way of Wisdom"?

Based on what we have said so far, it exists in the accumulation of knowledge, experience and an understanding of life, which we then apply into the situations we face each day. Therefore, the greater our knowledge and experience base is, the more likely we are to make a wise decision.

Whilst this is fundamentally true, there is another important dimension to the acquisition of wisdom, which is absolutely vital to the success of this process. To discover this, we need to explore and fully embrace what God has to say about the nature of wisdom, where wisdom comes from, and what our attitude towards it should be.

In the Bible God has given us a number of books traditionally called the "Wisdom literature", so let's begin there: Amongst them are some books that come primarily from the pen of King Solomon who is reputed to have been the wisest man who ever lived. They are called Proverbs, Ecclesiastes and Song of Solomon. He wasn't wise because he inherited good genes from his father David or because he studied hard, both of which may or may not be true. Instead, his great wisdom was given to him by God in response to a specific request for it. You see, even Solomon recognised he needed a wisdom for living that was greater than he could find in his own strength. So he turned to God, like we do as Christians today, and asked for *"a wise and discerning heart"* (1 Kings 3:9) to help him rule well. God replied by saying:

*"Since you have asked for this and not for long life or wealth for yourself, nor have asked for the death of your enemies but for discernment in administering justice, I will do what you have asked. **I will give you a wise and discerning heart**, so that there will never have been anyone like you, nor will there ever be."* (1 Kings 3:10-12)

It is worth noting that in asking for wisdom, he asked for the one thing that made all the other things he could have asked for safe. With wisdom he could safely handle great wealth without it corrupting him. And with wisdom he could enter treaties with other nations bringing economic and political peace across his kingdom. So God also said:

"Moreover, I will give you what you have not asked for—both wealth and honor—so that in your lifetime you will have no equal among kings. And if you walk in obedience to me and keep my decrees and commands as David your father did, I will give you a long life." (1 Kings 3:13-14)

This puts Solomon in a unique place when it comes to understanding what wisdom is and how to acquire it. So let's see what we can learn from him.

It's available

Solomon makes it clear that wisdom is available for everyone. Yes, even you.

The opening verses of the book of Proverbs, generally regarded as the best expression of Solomon's collected wisdom, says it is,

"...for gaining wisdom and instruction; for understanding words of insight; for receiving instruction in prudent behavior, doing what is right and just and fair; for giving prudence to those who are simple, knowledge and discretion to the young." (Proverbs 1:2-4)

That sounds to me exactly like what we are looking for! And it scoops up both the young and the simple, so if you are feeling you lack wisdom because of either, here is a source of hope for you.

He then makes the point that even if you think you already know it all and have sufficient wisdom, a characteristic of the wise is that they *"listen and add to their learning"* (Proverbs 1:5-6). So through the Scriptures written by Solomon, God makes available a level of wisdom needed by the young, the simple and the wise alike.

This means that wisdom is not the exclusive province of the rich, the powerful, the ruling classes or the best educated; it is available for all and is actually nothing to do with any of those categories. Some powerful people are fools and the way they exercise their power exposes their folly. Too many rich people squander their wealth, again showing their fundamental lack of wisdom. And even if you have had a private education, been to the best universities in the world and have a string of qualifications after your name, you can still be exposed as a fool when you start applying all that learning to the practical, everyday issues of life.

So, wisdom is definitely there for us but like Solomon, we too need to ask for it. In the New Testament, James makes the same point when he writes, *"If any of you lack wisdom, he should ask God who gives generously to all without finding fault, and it will be given to him"* (James 1:5). When they do, the evidence is seen *"by their good life, by deeds done in the humility that comes from wisdom"* (James 3:13).

If, however, the deeds of a person's life are instead characterised by *"envy and selfish ambition ... disorder and every evil practice"*, he makes it clear that such so-called "wisdom" does not come from God, but is *"earthly, unspiritual and demonic"* (James 3:14-16).

James pinpoints the fact that when you boil it all down, there are really just two sources of wisdom available for people to consult. There is the wisdom of this world, which seeks to find the best path without any reference to God, and there is the wisdom that comes from God – the one who created us, watches over us and loves to help us make great choices in life. And the contrast between the fruit of following each source of wisdom is pretty stark. In contrast to the *"earthly, unspiritual and demonic"* source of wisdom which produces *"envy and selfish ambition ... disorder and every evil practice"*, the *"wisdom that comes from heaven"* is characterised by being *"first of all pure; then peace-loving, considerate, submissive, full of mercy and good fruit, impartial and sincere"* (James 3:17).

I know which I would rather have! It is a no-brainer. I want the wisdom from heaven every time please.

However, every time I need that "bit of wisdom" it is not always clear which of the two sources it actually came from. Say I am in a bit of a quandary about a situation and my friend offers me "a bit of wisdom" to help with my dilemma. The question now becomes, which source is it from? It arrived in my world as the opinion of a concerned friend. And because I love them I am more likely to receive what they say as being *"wisdom from heaven"*. But it may actually be *"earthly, unspiritual"* wisdom that they have gathered on their journey, so should I therefore reject it? Aargh! Now I need wisdom to discern whether or not the wisdom offered is the kind of wisdom I want!

Before you get the impression that finding the way of

wisdom is complicated, let me make something very clear. Wisdom is not hard to understand. It is never so complicated and "deep" that you are unable to comprehend it. In fact, wisdom is characterised by its clarity not its obscurity. If you don't believe me, start reading Solomon's wisdom in the book of Proverbs. It is wonderfully simple, clear and practical. It does not confuse, it brings clarity, certainty and a sound basis from which to make great decisions.

This will become very clear as you set out on your search for wisdom and begin to recognise those two root sources of it. Over time you will develop the ability, with God's help, to discern in an instant whether a suggestion is from heaven or hell. It will become just part of your approach to life, a spiritual life-skill that keeps you on the path we might call "the way of wisdom".

Unfortunately, there is a school of thought that says that the more complicated a thing is to understand the wiser it must therefore be. But usually those who prize incomprehensibility are simply putting up a smoke-screen to cover their confusion and lack of true wisdom. So if you are of that school, leave it now. The wisdom that is available to us from heaven is not deep and baffling, it is clear and profoundly simple.

The search

Solomon makes it clear in his writings that true wisdom has to be searched for, which again could suggest it is "deep" and requires great intellectual study to attain. But that is not what he means. Rather he is saying that wisdom is not found lying around on the surface of life where you will just trip over it. No, it has to be dug for and searched out. There is a search required to find true wisdom and the search itself is all part of developing a character that is able to handle the wisdom once found.

Wisdom is like a diamond, only found deep in the earth

and requiring some excavation. Now, you can of course buy a diamond after someone else has done all the digging and searching, but you cannot purchase wisdom in quite the same way. "Yes you can," I hear some of you say, "I can find it in books and from the lives of great people." I would disagree. What you read about in books is the wisdom people accumulated from their search, their life-journey of pain and exploration. It is theirs and is safe in their hands because they paid the price for it. They have the marks from the digging all over their hands! For you to take their pearls of wisdom and call them yours is a deception; mere head knowledge, not true, experientially acquired wisdom. As a result, the wisdom will not bear the same fruit in your life as theirs.

Why read then? To be provoked to go on your own search for wisdom. What you read will guide you to the place where you eventually get a personal revelation about an issue. A word of wisdom will drop into your life like one of those diamonds. It will be like the proverbial light bulb coming on, a ray of hope will radiate through your soul and you will forever be in peace about the issue. You searched for and found wisdom appropriate for your personal situation. Nothing beats that feeling. It's yours forever.

Where it actually came from can be myriad. The Bible, great books, articles, sermons, observing people, noticing patterns of behaviour, and so on. But you and God went on a search and together you found that diamond ... you now know exactly how to manage little Jimmy's pocket money!

The lesson here is that wisdom has a way of giving itself to the true searcher, the one who is desperate enough to search it out rather than just waiting for it to appear. Because it never will just appear. The search itself reveals something about the quality of your soul, your true desire, and your capacity to handle the wisdom you eventually find.

That is why Solomon urges us to *"turn your ear to wisdom ... call out for insight and cry aloud for understanding, and if you look for it as for silver and search for it as for hidden treasure, then you will ... find the knowledge of God. For the Lord gives wisdom; from his mouth come knowledge and understanding"* (Proverbs 2:1-6).

He pinpoints that the search will always take us to God because for us, it is the "wisdom from heaven" we seek. We go on a journey with God, to God. And on our personal journey with him we unearth the nuggets of wisdom we need for today. After we have found them he says:

"Then you will understand what is right and just and fair—every good path. For wisdom will enter your heart, and knowledge will be pleasant to your soul. Discretion will protect you, and understanding will guard you. Wisdom will save you from the ways of wicked men" (Proverbs 2:9-12).

Remember Jesus taught his followers to, *"Ask and keep on asking, knock and keep on knocking, seek and keep on seeking"* (Matthew 7:7 Amplified). He encouraged them to search for wisdom to live life well. In fact he also chose to disguise truth in parables so that only those who really sought it out would find it. Was that unfair? Shouldn't his wisdom be dispersed freely to all?

No, because the non-searching soul does not have the capacity to hold and use such a treasure.

The search builds into the seeker a capacity to handle wisdom once it is acquired. It makes them responsible, mature, grateful and protective of this diamond of truth. It is like the chicken that has to hack its way out of the egg; it gains strength through the process. To reduce the struggle would potentially destroy the life being shaped by it. Quite a thought.

Just think about our money-driven, get-rich-quick world of lotteries and gambling to see an example of this. Wealth steadily accumulated through hard work seldom destroys people – the journey develops wisdom to handle it. But the lottery winner who suddenly gets rich quick is often destroyed by their lack of wisdom in handling the wealth. That destruction may be financial, relational or emotional. As we noted earlier, Solomon's quest for wisdom qualified him to handle great wealth and the same applies to everyone.

Yes, wisdom is available, but it has to be searched for. That desperate search may take us through difficulty, doubts, fears and trials of all kinds. But it is doing a work in us that will prepare us to be worthy recipients of the wisdom from heaven for everyday life on earth. It is a price worth paying every time.

Chapter 4
Hello Wisdom

So far we have established that wisdom is available if you will earnestly seek it out, and that the search itself will equip you to handle wisdom when you find it. But, be honest, as yet do you know what it is you are actually looking for? What does the "wisdom from heaven" actually look like? You know there is a "way of wisdom" that is the best path in life to follow, but what does that way really look like? And how will you know when you have found it?

This is where you will need to make a concept shift. I suspect you are looking for a set of guidelines for life or a particular aspect of it. I would, therefore, guess that you expect wisdom to look like a set of proverbial maxims or a code to live by – so you are looking for words, rules, a guidebook, or a person who seems to have such a set of guidelines you can learn from. And in many ways wisdom does eventually look like that, but not to begin with. Before that, you need to meet Wisdom.

Let me introduce you to Wisdom. Not a concept, a set of proverbial maxims or a code for living but a person. Wisdom is a person. Grasping this is crucial to your search for the "wisdom from heaven" because until you meet Wisdom personally, you can never walk fully in his ways.

Solomon was the first to point us down the path of searching for a person, rather than a set of wise sayings, in our pursuit of wisdom. The first nine chapters of his book of Proverbs are written in the form of a letter of advice from a father to a son. Some commentators have actually called this preamble before the main collection of Solomon's Proverbs, "The Way of Wisdom". In it, the father figure assures the young man that wisdom is certainly available if he will just search for it and then fully embrace it. So, we can imagine the young man setting out on his quest, much like we do. Solomon then gathers what James later describes as the "wisdom from heaven" and the "wisdom of this world" into two people who each call out to the young man, encouraging him to follow their ways. The two characters are women, one called Wisdom and one called Folly.

So the issue becomes, will the young man follow Wisdom or Folly?

First we hear from Wisdom. What she has to say is both a corrective to foolish, self-destructive behaviour patters and an invitation to walk with her and heed her advice. It is Wisdom who urges us to fear God and to walk in close relationship with him (2:1-8), which will bless and protect us. Through the following chapters she goes on to say things like,

"Whoever listens to me will live in safety and be at ease, without fear of harm (1:33) ... Wisdom will save you from the ways of wicked men, from men whose words are perverse (2:12) ... Do not forsake wisdom, and she will protect you; love her, and she will watch over you ... Cherish her, and she will exalt you; embrace her, and she will honour you. She will give you a garland to grace your head and present you with a glorious crown." (4:5-9)

Wisdom presents us with a wonderfully God-centred attitude

to life; a life characterised by knowledge, understanding and wisdom that will flow through us in blessing to others and ourselves. Every verse is packed with truth to live by, but not as a rule or law, rather as a relational expression of love for God and a love for this person, Wisdom.

By contrast we then meet the second woman, Folly. She is an adulteress, unfaithful to her husband and looking to lure young men into illicit nights of pleasure. It is a wonderfully poetic way of describing the temptations that come our way from the "wisdom of this world". She lures the young man into her lifestyle:

"With persuasive words she led him astray; she seduced him with her smooth talk. All at once he followed her like an ox going to the slaughter, like a deer stepping into a noose." (7:21-22)

Like Wisdom, Folly has set herself up in a prominent place where she can call out to those she seeks to ensnare in her schemes (9:14). We read:

"Folly is an unruly woman ... calling out to those who pass by ... 'Let all who are simple come to my house!' To those who have no sense she says, 'Stolen water is sweet; food eaten in secret is delicious!' But little do they know that the dead are there, that her guests are deep in the realm of the dead." (9:13-18)

To follow Folly is therefore to follow a path which leads ultimately to death, the absolute opposite to the path of Wisdom that leads to life and fruitfulness. No wonder then, that Wisdom says of Folly:

"Do not let your heart turn to her ways or stray into her paths. Many are the victims she has brought down; her slain are a mighty throng. Her house is a highway to the grave, leading down to the chambers of death." (7:25-27)

It is inescapable that these two women totally personify the two types of wisdom described by James in the New Testament: "wisdom from heaven" and "wisdom of this world" (James

3:13-17). One is totally positive, life-giving and carries the hallmark of heaven. The other is negative, ungodly and at root source, demonic. As such, it leads those who follow it into death.

This opens up our thinking to the possibility that the way of wisdom we seek is actually rooted in a relationship with a person. We don't just love what Wisdom says, we love Wisdom herself. We embrace her, walk in her ways and choose to be guided by her.

Shadow to substance

All this is an Old Testament pointer to a New testament reality we enjoy as Christians today, because we cannot escape the thought that this woman Wisdom sounds a lot like someone else we know. Just consider how she describes herself and ask yourself who else comes to mind:

"I was formed long ages ago, at the very beginning, when the world came to be... I was there when he set the heavens in place, when he marked out the horizon on the face of the deep, when he established the clouds above and fixed securely the fountains of the deep ... Then I was constantly at his side. I was filled with delight day after day, rejoicing always in his presence, rejoicing in his whole world and delighting in mankind." (8:22-31)

Who can this be alluding to but Jesus? The one of whom John said, *"He was with God in the beginning. Through him all things were made; without him nothing was made that has been made"* (John 1:2-3). In fact, the more you think about the person Wisdom in Proverbs, the more you will be directed to Jesus.[1]

The "way of wisdom" you seek, is the "way of Christ". We all came to Christ because we were seeking wisdom to

---

1. See Appendix for more examples of the relationship between the person Wisdom and Jesus.

navigate this life successfully. Along the way to this conclusion we discovered that the "wisdom of this world" is actually foolishness when compared to the wisdom of God revealed in Christ (1 Corinthians 1:18-25). So we responded to *"Christ … the wisdom of God"* (1 Corinthians 1:24).

We are now *"in Christ Jesus, who has become for us wisdom from God"* (1 Corinthians 1:30). He is Wisdom and we are in him! And right there is the source of the "way of wisdom" you seek on all and every matter in life.

Jesus is the *"Word made flesh"* (John 1:14); the Wisdom of Proverbs fleshed out and imparted to us by the Holy Spirit. No wonder Paul says *"My purpose is that … they may know Christ, in whom are hidden all the treasures of wisdom and knowledge"* (Colossians 2:2-3). Note, they are hidden in Christ, so the search must take us deeper into a relationship with Jesus.

Think again about James' words: *"But the wisdom that comes from heaven is first of all pure; then peace-loving, considerate, submissive, full of mercy and good fruit, impartial and sincere"* .(James 3:17).

The New Testament writers are simply joining the dots from the Old Testament to the New. The prophets had declared the Messiah *"will be the sure foundation for your times, a rich store of salvation and wisdom and knowledge"* (Isaiah 33:6).

So for us to search for wisdom is to search for Jesus. Not just for his teaching, but for him. Not just for a wise saying, but for relationship. We don't pursue knowledge, understanding or education, we seek Christ, to know him more intimately, to understand his ways and to share in his wisdom. Our aim is to become more like Jesus, to be *"transformed into his likeness with ever increasing glory"* (2 Corinthians 3:18).

The Way of Wisdom is the Way of Christ. He is therefore the starting point of our search for any "bit of wisdom" we need for life today. That is why I have confidently called this book

Wisdom Wins! Jesus has already defeated Satan, sin, death and hell through the cross. He does not just win in the end, he has already won! And you are "in Christ" if you have made him your Lord and saviour. You are "in Wisdom" and therefore have access to the winning strategy for life.

In the second part of this book we get practical, very practical. But you will soon see that everyday practical wisdom is rooted in Jesus. So my prayer for you is that you *"may know Christ, in whom are hidden all the treasures of wisdom and knowledge"* (Colossians 2:2-3) more deeply than you have ever known him before.

Ours is a journey into Jesus, the one who is Wisdom … and that *Wisdom Wins!*

Chapter 5
Starting Right

I hope you are now seeing why so many people fail to find the wisdom they want. They are simply looking in the wrong place!

Once you have grasped that Jesus is the essence and source of the wisdom from heaven you are looking for, the way you search for it will change. No longer will you search for helpful facts, keys to turn or principles to apply. They will come, but first you will search for a close relationship with Jesus. It will also change the people you speak to in your search for wisdom. No longer will it just be those who seem to know a lot, or who have had experience in life, it will first be those who are devoted followers of Christ; who love God, his Word and his ways. People close to Jesus have access to all the wisdom that he has to offer for life.

Your fundamental attitude to God is therefore very important to your search for wisdom. Christians believe that Jesus is God, one person of the divine unity of Father, Son and Holy Spirit we call the Godhead or Trinity. So to deepen your relationship with Jesus is to deepen your relationship with your heavenly Father and the Holy Spirit too. They are indivisible.

What do you think about God?

What comes into your mind when you think about God? Come to that, what comes into your mind when someone says "Jesus" or "The Holy Spirit"? This is very important because if you have a faulty belief about God, your ability to receive wisdom from him is limited.

I do not have the space here to explain fully how wonderful God reveals himself to be. But suffice to say, he is our creator so understands us completely and utterly. He is eternal, so stands outside of time and knows not only our past but also our future. He made us in his image and gave us the awesome power of a free will, so he understands the dilemmas we face about how to exercise that free will as we navigate life. He loves us without reservation but will never force us to love him back. To have moral worth our love for God must always be a free choice and is part of our search for the wisdom that flows from him. He is also holy and resists all that contradicts his holiness, so we quickly become aware of the distinction between good and evil as we walk close to him. His holiness is expressed by his righteousness and justice, which characterise all he does. He is also described as being light and therefore exposes darkness, so we soon learn to distinguish the wisdom from heaven from the wisdom of this world.

Ours is therefore a relational search not a factual search. As we grow in our personal relationship with God we begin to understand how God thinks, how God acts and what pleases him. We discover that there are consequences too. When we violate his wise ways, we experience pain and difficulty in life. Sometimes we are even disciplined by our heavenly Father, which can be painful at the time, but which always leads to a helpful correction in our behaviour and a deep sense of peace as we discover more about the wisdom of living life God's way (Hebrews 12:6-11).

We develop what the Bible writers call a healthy "fear of the Lord". This is not a blind, irrational fear of God, which makes us quake in our boots because God is an overbearing monster who loves to punish us – that would show we have a completely wrong understanding of what God is like. Instead, it is a reverential, healthy fear of not wanting to take a single step outside of the way of wisdom from heaven. It is rooted in a growing understanding of who God is, how he has made us and the best way to live life.

The fear of the Lord is like the healthy fear children have of displeasing their father who they know loves them completely and utterly. They know Dad will discipline them, if needed, to teach them how to live wisely, so they avoid the things that displease him and, by doing so, automatically walk in the way of wisdom. So, walking in a healthy "fear of Dad" helps them choose to do what is right, avoid evil and keep living wisely. That's how it is with us and God. In fact, Solomon says that *"The Fear of The Lord teaches a man wisdom"* (Proverbs 15:33) and that *"Through the fear of the Lord, evil is avoided"* (Proverbs 16:6). This healthy, reverential respect for God keeps us on the right path.

That is why the Bible writers say: *"The fear of the LORD is the beginning of wisdom, and knowledge of the Holy One is understanding"* (Proverbs 9:10). It all starts with this base attitude. If you want to enjoy the blessed life of walking in the wisdom of heaven, you must learn to live in a healthy fear of the Lord, which comes from gaining a true understanding of who God is and how he relates to you.

That takes time because all relationships develop over time as you do life together. They can't always be rushed. It also takes effort, self-sacrifice and a willingness to learn about God from the Bible, other Christians, books you read and studies you perform. But the time and effort are just part of the search for wisdom we explained earlier.

Learned and revealed

In my experience, the fear of the Lord is both learned and revealed. I was first taught it by my parents who loved God and did their best to bring me up according to the principles of God's Word. Along the way I learned about God, his nature and how to life a life in accordance with the wisdom from heaven. But it was all head knowledge at that stage. Only when I started making personal choices about how to handle my relationships, what to think about, how to do my work, spend my money and so on, did that knowledge start to slip from my head to my heart. Along the way I made some poor choices and felt the disapproval of my heavenly Father, until eventually the light bulb came on. In that moment I had a revelation, a personal realisation about the true nature of God and how to walk his wise ways, and I chose it. I chose to walk in the wisdom of heaven. Now what keeps me forever on that path is a healthy fear of the Lord which I first "learned" from others, but which had to become a personal revelation, borne out of my desperate search for wisdom to live by.

This is why the Bible instructs us to first teach people to fear the Lord. Parents should teach it to their children (Deuteronomy 6:2), spiritual leaders like Moses were commanded to teach it to their people (Deuteronomy 10:12) and the prophets who mentored the kings of Israel instructed them to fear God (2 Chronicles 26:1-6). This teaching is basically telling people who God is, what he is like and how to relate to him. But then they have to put it to the test and walk with God personally. Only then do they gain a revelation that what they have been taught is true. All uncertainty then leaves them. What they know about God, they really and truly know experientially. It is in both their head and their heart.

This, then, is our proper starting point on the journey towards finding wisdom: *"The fear of the LORD is the beginning of wisdom, and knowledge of the Holy One is understanding"* (Proverbs 9:10).

As we close this introductory, foundation-laying section of this book, please take some time to reflect on your relationship with Jesus. It truly is the key to finding the wisdom you seek. There is no true wisdom outside of a close, living and personal relationship with him.

If you have grasped all we have explored so far...

- that this complex world sends us all on a search for the "way of wisdom"

- that wisdom has only two basic sources – heaven and hell

- that it is available to you, but has to be searched for earnestly

- that your search is first for the person who is Wisdom, Jesus Christ

- who you approach with healthy, reverential fear

... I am confident that you are on the way to a successful search for the wisdom from heaven.

You are on course to discover that *Wisdom Wins!*

Part 2:
The Way of Wisdom

"By wisdom a house is built."
(Proverbs 24:3-4)

*"Wisdom has built her house;
she has set up its seven pillars."*
(Proverbs 9:1)

Introduction:

Let's get practical.

The way of wisdom is essentially the way of Jesus. He is the *"wisdom from heaven"* (James 3:17). He is the *"word made flesh"* (John 1:14) and as such fleshed out all the wisdom of the character of the same name in Solomon's writings. He is the one who *"has become for us wisdom from God"* (1 Corinthians 1:30).

So it is to Jesus we first turn as we search for wisdom, confident that *"In Christ ... are hidden all the treasures of wisdom and knowledge"* (Colossians 2:2-3).

This relational search for wisdom will inevitably take us into the teachings of Jesus, but I am going to use Solomon's character, Wisdom, to create a more visual framework for the next few chapters of our exploration.

At one point in the poetic imagery, Solomon describes the character Wisdom making an invitation to her house, a house she has built on seven pillars (9:1). The number seven in Scripture is often significant, being symbolic of completion or perfection. So, hers is a well-built, complete house that will not fall down. Seven pillars, the perfect number, are supporting it.

As we study all that Solomon writes about wisdom in the Bible, we soon discover that there are some very strong themes, which seem to unite and characterise the life of wisdom he is promoting – the life we all want. It is those themes we will be homing in on. And I am suggesting there are seven of them – seven themes that are like pillars which, if built into the "house" of your life, will ensure it is the home of Wisdom.

As we said previously, life is complicated and there are certainly more than seven issues we have to navigate along the way of wisdom. But I believe these seven themes form the bulk of it and that they have a voice into all the other situations we face in life. In them is enshrined the "wisdom from heaven" for life on earth today and their principles will guide you through the complexities of everyday living with skill and wisdom. Get these in place and your roof certainly won't fall in! In fact, far from it, get these in place and Wisdom will have moved in.

So, on the foundation of a healthy fear of the Lord, which is a proper attitude towards Jesus, we construct the seven pillars. Together they build Wisdom's House.

WISDOM'S HOUSE

A PROPER ATTITUDE TOWARDS

JESUS
'The fear of the Lord'

WISDOM'S HOUSE

Teachability

A PROPER ATTITUDE TOWARDS

JESUS

'The fear of the Lord'

Chapter 6
TEACHABILITY:
The Wisdom of Being a Learner for Life

Some years ago we had a family holiday in Scotland, based near Fort William in the Highlands, a beautiful part of the world. It rained. A lot.

One evening I took one of my boys down to the waterside in the persistent drizzle to do some fishing. As he was sat on the quayside spinning for mackerel, I sat in the car keeping dry and an amazing thing happened, the sun came out! It was glorious. The skies suddenly cleared and the early evening sun bathed the surrounding hills with a warm glow. I jumped out of the car to take it all in then reached for my binoculars and began panning the far side of the loch and mountainsides with some delight.

It then dawned on me. Behind me was Ben Nevis, the highest mountain in Scotland, and as yet we had not seen it without a cloudy summit. So I turned to take in its magnificence. But from where I stood I was not able to get a clear sight of the summit. Somewhat frustrated, I began looking for possible places from which I could get a better view. And I spotted the ideal one. The view from the little cluster of cottages I could see across the Loch from me would be spectacular. I estimated it was about half a mile away across the water. All I needed to do was nip over that short stretch of water.

Out came the map book. Where was the nearest bridge? Well, if you know Scotland you will know the answer, there isn't one! The only way to get to that ideal viewpoint was to drive around the loch, a journey of 28 miles. Such is travel in Scotland. Oh how I wished for a speedboat or a helicopter to zip me across for a quick look. But it was not to be. The only way I could get to the destination I desired was by taking the long road and I was not willing to make the journey.

I think the Christian life is a lot like that. It is a journey filled with promise and has a glorious destination. Once saved, we are immediately included in all that it means to be a Christian: we are free from sin, in a new family, now ruling in life, and a completely new creation. But enjoying the reality of all of this requires us to go on a journey with Jesus, to grow in understanding, change in behaviour and increasingly become more like Christ as we *"press on towards the goal"* (Philippians 3:14). We are very aware we have *"everything we need for life and godliness"* in Christ (2 Peter 1:3), but that we must make it a fleshed-out reality by practical Christian living. Our amazing status in Christ has to become our actual state as a believer today – and that takes time and process. It is the journey of the Christian life, the process of sanctification, the path to becoming more like Jesus. It is the "way of wisdom".

Now, be honest. How often have you been like me on that loch-side and wished there was a short cut to becoming wiser or more like Jesus? I certainly have, many times. But the fact is, we need to take the journey.

The journey teaches us and prepares us for what is coming further up the road – which only God knows. So to try and take a short cut would leave us badly unprepared and ill equipped for things we have to deal with up the road.

I believe this is why Solomon repeatedly instructs those on the way of wisdom to remain teachable. He understood that living a wise life requires us to travel each stage of the journey thoroughly, learning all it has to teach us along the way. In this way we gather wisdom as we travel. And we gather it in the order God leads us in.

In his wisdom – because remember, Jesus is Wisdom – he leads us through each twist in the road of life for our overall benefit. We may not understand why we are having to learn a lot of patience right now, or having to humble ourselves in this season, or have a strong desire to be equipped in a certain way. But God does. So take your time, be teachable and learn all that you know God is trying to teach you about right now.

I'm sure the 28 mile drive around the loch in Scotland would have been interesting. There would have been new sights to see, people to meet, places to explore and experiences to enrich my life. But I was not willing to make that journey, so I may have missed out. And that was OK in the scheme of things that evening. But in the bigger scheme of my Christian life and my desire to walk each day in the wisdom from heaven, it would not be all right.

For you to become the fullness of all that Jesus has made you to be, demands you travel the journey with all its ups and downs, learning every step of the way from Wisdom, your wonderful teacher. The moment you stop learning is the moment your journey into wisdom ends. No speedboat or helicopter shortcuts are allowed.

So, just how teachable are you? Here are three qualities Solomon identifies as being characteristic of someone who understands the wisdom of being a life-long learner:

1. They Want to Learn

A deep desire to learn new things is fundamental to growing in wisdom. Maybe you think that's stating the obvious, but lots of people want to have wisdom without going through the learning process required to get it. They want the product without the process.

Whereas, healthy learners love the learning process itself. They relish each and every day and the learning opportunities it brings their way. It becomes an attitude to life, which positions them as candidates to learn far more than their more passive friends. Some people just learn from what is put under their nose, but life-long learners on a search for wisdom don't stop there. They start there and then press for more knowledge.

Faced with a new situation they don't panic or back down, they embrace it as a learning opportunity. This grows them in many ways. They grow:

- intellectually because they may do research
- relationally because they will ask other skilled people about their challenge
- emotionally because it may ignite their passions or expose their fears
- spiritually because they will be talking to God a lot about it, and,
- experientially because they are practically dealing with it

See how rich they have become by embracing a new learning opportunity. This desire to learn sets them up to prosper. As

Solomon says, *"Whoever gives heed to instruction prospers"* (Proverbs 16:20). It also demonstrates a degree of previously acquired wisdom because *"the wise listen and add to their learning, and the discerning get guidance"* (Proverbs 1:5).

Learning is an active process. Just because you are in a classroom does not mean you will learn anything – ask any school teacher! The student must engage with the learning environment they are in. It is the same in all spheres of life. Marriage and family life are learning environments we have to engage with positively to learn from and grow in. So is your workplace, leisure activity and local church. Just being there does not mean you will learn a thing. You must be there with an attitude that says "I want to learn" and become tenacious about it.

Even being one of the twelve disciples around Jesus did not guarantee a common learning outcome for them all. Just compare where Judas, Peter and John each ended up. But in among them was one disciple who, for me, stands out as a teachable, life-long learner. He engaged with Jesus in a way the others did not and so learned a lot more than most, which equipped him to play a particularly significant part in the church when it emerged. That disciple is Simon Peter.

If you examine all the conversations between Jesus and his disciples it is usually Peter who is asking the questions and pushing the boundaries. For example:

- Jesus spoke in parables the disciples did not always understand and it is invariably Peter who asks, *"Explain the parable to us"* (Matthew 15:15) and on another occasion he asked, *"Lord, are you telling this parable to us, or to everyone?"* (Luke 12:41).
- Once Jesus taught them about forgiveness. They all nodded politely as if they understood, except Peter who asked, *"Lord, how many times shall I forgive my brother*

when he sins against me? Up to seven times?" (Matthew 18:21). What followed was a further teaching from Jesus; one they would never had received without Peter pressing for practical wisdom.

• When Jesus cursed the fig tree, all the disciples heard him. But the next day it was Peter who pointed out it had happened (Mark 11:20). He was observant.

• All the disciples went quiet as Jesus took a towel and started washing their feet. It was one of those pregnant silences because this seemed all wrong; the master washing the disciples feet? Until he got to Peter (John 13:8-9) and then we learn what was going on as Jesus responded to Peter.

How proactive is your learning process? To walk in the way of wisdom it will need to be very active, like Peter's. I would challenge to you to be inquisitive and ask questions; don't be too naively accepting of things people put under your nose. Remember, just because its on TV doesn't mean it's true or correct! Press for more information so you get a true understanding of things, people and events. Be observant. Notice things, people and patterns in life. Push the boundaries and dare to ask the questions everyone wants to ask, but no one dare!

Do it in church too. We all love our pastors and spiritual leaders; they are our friends and many have become spiritual parents to us too. But they are all human, have personal opinions and can sometimes get things wrong – like we all do. So be like the Christians in a town called Berea who Paul commended because, after he had spoken, they went away and *"examined the scriptures daily to see if these things were true"* (Acts 17:11).

It will involve reading, thinking, talking, listening, watching and a good deal of discussion no doubt. But the life-long learner in you will gather the wisdom it needs from this point of the journey.

This process never ends. *"Instruct the wise and they will be wiser still"* (Proverbs 9:9) says Solomon. Being a teachable, learner for life characterises the wise because they have understood that they must never retire, level off or graduate from the learning process required to travel the way of wisdom.

2. They Welcome Correction

Now to a less palatable point. It is true that a deep desire to learn characterises the wise, but to attain true wisdom they also need an equally strong desire to be corrected. In fact, they must love it. *"Rebuke the wise and they will love you"* (Proverbs 9:8) says Solomon.

The wise love correction because it helps them on their journey. In fact, Solomon puts it quite bluntly by saying *"Whoever hates correction is stupid"* (Proverbs 12:1). You can't get clearer than that. A true learner welcomes correction. But the know-it-all despises correction.

The measure of wisdom in a truly teachable person leads them to understand that if they are wrong in their conclusions or opinions, and then start instructing others, they are actually leading them astray. This is the weighty responsibility of being a teacher, which the New Testament warns must be carried soberly (James 3:1). The teacher must therefore be open to correction more than most. As Solomon pointed out, *"Whoever ignores correction leads others astray"* (Proverbs 10:17), something none of us want to do.

Now, you may think to yourself, "I'm not a teacher," to avoid this one. But before you do, just reflect on the people in your sphere of influence in life: family, friends, the new Christians who look up to you, work colleagues and so on. You may never stand up and teach them from behind a pulpit, but you teach them every day when you express an opinion or offer them advice. So when correction comes your way, take it. In fact, love it and warmly thank the people helping you because ultimately *"whoever heeds correction is honoured"* (Proverbs 13:18).

Of course, our ability to welcome correction is related to the manner in which it comes. If it is in the form of a snide remark, criticism or other form of put-down, we are less likely to receive it. In fact we are more likely to become dogmatic about our position and end up in a stand-off. But if it comes from a warm, loving friend who walks close to Jesus, we are good with it.

All I will say is that whoever correction comes through, have the grace and stature to at least weigh it. Don't let your pride or reputation get in the way of what could be divine correction. The prophet Balaam was corrected by a donkey, which he didn't appreciate at all until God gave the donkey a voice so he could explain himself. Balaam then had to repent and swallow his pride because the donkey was right (Numbers 22:21-34).

One of the things you will sometimes be corrected by are your own mistakes. Isn't it horrible? You are trying your best to follow Jesus, learn all you can and put it into practice, but it all goes wrong. You fall flat on your face and begin to wonder if you wouldn't be better settling for staying where you are on the road. We have all been there.

Mistakes are great learning opportunities and a great corrective. Sometimes it is the sheer pain of the mistake that pushes you through to do better and go further. I think a robust attitude to being corrected by his own mistakes is what we see in Peter once again. Maybe it was because he was such a committed learner that he made so many? After all, it does seem that those who are corrected the least, are those who do the least.

I like to look at it this way. The more effort I make to learn, the more attempts I make to succeed and, therefore, mistakes I inevitably make, the more opportunity I give God to help me through those mistakes.

That was certainly Peter's experience.

- He walked on water. Amazing! But then took his eye off Jesus and began to sink. Big mistake. But Jesus reached out and caught him and taught him a lesson about faith (Matthew 14:30-31).

- Later, he blatantly denied even knowing Jesus on three occasions, just as Jesus had warned him. Big mistake. And it drove him to tears of repentance (Matthew 26:75). But then Jesus created a wonderful opportunity for him to verbalise his love for him three times and set things right (John 21:15-17). The lessons he learned about himself and the grace of Jesus towards him must have been invaluable.

- After Christ's ascension he was still prejudiced against the Gentiles (non-Jews). So he only took the Gospel to fellow Jews. Big mistake. So God corrected him through a vision and sent him to be the first preacher to the Gentiles (Acts 10). Quite an object lesson to correct his theology.

- And some years later Paul had to have another word with him about this same issue (Galatians 2:11-14). Ouch! Sometimes we need to be corrected more than once on an issue, but we must still welcome it and allow it to keep us walking firmly in the way of wisdom.

One important thing shines through all these examples of people being corrected: it was God who was doing the correcting. Wisdom himself was helping the person learn how to walk in his ways. And that is what makes it such a positive experience. Jesus never corrects us in a way that destroys us. He corrects us like a loving father. He will be firm and clear, but always loving to the core.

The Bible teaches us that God – or Wisdom – corrects his people in three main ways.

1. By the inner witness of the *Holy Spirit*. Because the spirit of Christ lives in us, he directs us from within as we navigate the journey of the Christian life. So generally, the first person to tell us we have made a mistake or done wrong is the spirit of Wisdom within us. We feel it as a pang of conscience or maybe just a deep sense in our heart that we have gone wrong. So if we walk closely with the Holy Spirit, we will be very alert to his corrections to our thoughts, speech, attitudes and behaviour. It is like having a teacher inside us (John 14:26) who leads us constantly into the truth of the way of wisdom (John 16:13).

2. Through the *Bible* which is the Word of God. One of its functions is to correct us: *"All Scripture is God-breathed and is useful for teaching, rebuking, correcting and training in righteousness, so that the servant of God may be thoroughly equipped for every good work"* (2 Timothy 3:16-17). As we read the Bible it corrects us in harmony and cooperation with the Holy Spirit who lives in us. So together they are a powerful corrective to help us learn to walk in the way of wisdom.

3. Through the *Body of Christ*, which consists of every believer we are outworking our Christianity alongside. We are told by Paul to *"Let the word of Christ dwell among you richly as you teach and admonish one another with all wisdom"* (Colossians 3:16). So within the fellowship of believers there is a third corrective that is also linked directly to the Bible – the word of Christ – from where the principles of wisdom flow.

I hope you are beginning to understand that loving correction is potentially a life saver! It is God's gracious provision to keep you walking in the way of wisdom and progressing in your Christian life. So, keep cultivating a love of correction alongside your deep desire to learn. Then you will also be heeding the warning Wisdom gives to those who ignore her advice:

"At the end of your life you will groan,
when your flesh and body are spent.
You will say, 'How I hated discipline!
How my heart spurned correction!
I would not obey my teachers
or turn my ear to my instructors.
And I was soon in serious trouble
in the assembly of God's people.'"
(Proverbs 5:11-14)

3. They are Activists not Theorists

There is one final characteristic of the truly teachable, learner for life that we must highlight: they are always willing to act, to try things, to have a go. They know that ultimately a thing is not truly learned until it is acted on. So they are activists, not just theorists.

The wise are busy, because wisdom does not exist in intellectual concepts alone, it exists in action. James explained what those actions look like when he said, *"Who is wise and understanding among you? Let them show it by their good life, by deeds done in the humility that comes from wisdom"* (James 3:13). So the ultimate aim of the person seeking wisdom, is to live "a good life" characterised by deeds that flow from the wisdom they have humbly learned. That sounds simple – and it is. Remember, we established earlier that wisdom is not complicated or confusing it is clear and profoundly simple.

Jesus made the same point. He said, *"Wisdom is proved right by her deeds"* (Matthew 11:19). So, as a measure of whether you are wise or not, he is not primarily interested in what you know in your head or feel in your heart, but what the actions of your life display. For they flow from your mind and heart, they are the tangible evidence of your wisdom.

Earlier in this chapter we talked about our desire to take

shortcuts on the way of wisdom, helicopter rides that whisk us past difficult terrain or hazards we don't like the look of. Often that desire is simply to avoid the work we know we'll have to put in to genuinely learn the wisdom we seek. But we have been seeing that such shortcuts are counter productive. The truly teachable person, one characterised by being a life long learner, has a deep desire to learn from every stage of the journey and welcomes any corrections that come their way. That will look like them being rather busy!

Jesus told a story which illustrates this point. We call it the parable of the Prodigal Son (Luke 15:11-31). This young man thought he knew it all and that he had it all. So took his inheritance early. A big mistake. The subsequent journey proved him wrong and he lost everything. Eventually he found himself in a terrible situation that acted as a corrective to get him back onto the way of wisdom and a journey back to his loving father. My question is, at what point in the narrative do we really know he had found the wisdom he needed from this episode?

• Was it when we read, *"When he came to his senses, he said, 'How many of my father's hired servants have food to spare, and here I am starving to death!'"* (v17). No, I don't think so. We often have a mental realisation that we, or things, need to change and it gets no further than our head.

• Or was it when he then says, *"I will set out and go back to my father and say to him: Father, I have sinned against heaven and against you. I am no longer worthy to be called your son; make me like one of your hired servants"* (v18-19). No, there is still no evidence of tangible wisdom having arrived in his life. How many of us do exactly what he did and then never give the speech?

• Or was it when we read, *"So he got up and went to his father"* (v20). Yes! This is the first visible action that displays his new-found wisdom.

The wise are activists not theorists.

Their wisdom is tangible and exists in the good deeds they perform, the great choices they make and positive life they lead. People like that are teachable, learners for life.

Is the pillar in place?

It's time for an honesty moment. If one of Solomon's seven pillars of wisdom is to be teachable, a life-long learner, you need to be actively constructing that pillar. So:

- What are you learning right now?
- What are you reading, watching and listening to?
- What skills are you developing?
- What new people are you developing life-enriching relationships with?

Think through the various learning environments of your life and ask yourself, what am I learning in my marriage, family life, parenting, work life, church life, social life … and any others you can identify.

Have the courage and commitment to take the time to learn, be humble enough welcome much needed correction when it comes, and get busy outworking the wisdom you have found by living a *"good life"* characterised by *"deeds done in the humility that comes from wisdom"* (James 3:13).

WISDOM'S HOUSE

Diligence

A PROPER ATTITUDE TOWARDS

JESUS
'The fear of the Lord'

Chapter 7
DILIGENCE:
The Wisdom of Working Hard

In my school days I was never top of the class. But then, neither was I bottom. Instead I seemed to always be somewhere in the middle, the epitome of average. School reports would say "Stephen tried hard" and occasionally "he could do better". But generally I plodded through my studies, trying my best yet never achieving the accolade of being an "A-star" student.

My wonderful parents had the measure of me and assured me that as long as I consistently did my best, it was sufficient. My Dad would say, "Play the long game son; just stick at it and do the best you can each day." So I did. But some things about the seeming inequalities of the whole educational process really annoyed me.

For a start there was Michael Sharpe. He was very clever, but lazy. Somehow he managed to get straight A's even though he spent many a school day shirking classes to pursue his hobby of horse racing – not riding them, betting on them! He studied form, followed the races every day and would often nip out of school on some pretence to listen to races on the radio. We all knew he did it because he boasted about it. He even had an uncle who placed bets for him because he was under age. Then along came the exams and he would cram for them and come top! That really annoyed me.

But as life goes, we eventually left school and moved on into adult life. Many of my friends went off to University, but because my grades were only average, I decided to stay local, take a job as a Trainee Chartered Surveyor and, at the ripe old age of 19, married the love of my life.

My route into the surveying profession was regarded as the "long route" because most entered as graduates. But I had chosen to train while working, which involved day release visits to college and a large amount of personal study by correspondence to prepare me for the annual exams. We had to qualify within 10 years of starting and I later learned that the pass rate was only 4% for students like me.

Two years in I started a new college for my day release course and who should be there but Michael Sharpe. I was very surprised. He had dropped out of university and taken a trainee position like mine, so once again we were aiming for the same qualification. But this time I had the edge, not because I was more intelligent than him, but because I had better motivation. Michael was still working for money to spend on the horses and his cramming skills were far less relevant in the continuous learning environment we were in. Whereas I had my wife and our first child to support. My eyes were to the future. So I got my head down and applied myself diligently to my studies, for my family and our future. Evening after evening I studied and plodded my way through to full qualification in just over 5 years and its subsequent rewards. Sadly, Michael never made it, and as far as I know he is still professionally unqualified despite his high potential.

Looking back on it, diligence was the only difference between us. Diligence plays the long game rather than trying to find success through a short burst of input, energy or application to the task. And my godly parents had instilled that attitude into me for which I am forever grateful.

Now, many years later, I am convinced that my experience is common. I see it everywhere. It is the diligent who succeed. The diligent can be seen building great businesses, families and churches. They play the long game, their careful, persistent effort moving them through obstacles and challenges to establish their goal. And that diligence contributes greatly to the longevity of what they have worked so consistently hard to achieve.

Solomon saw it too

For clarity, diligence is best defined as "careful and persistent work or effort". It is to be conscientious, faithful and reliable in your application to a task.

I now realise that what I am seeing is what Solomon saw too. Throughout his writings he comments on the merits of being diligent and the dangers of not being so. And for that reason I am lifting it out as a "pillar of wisdom" for us to explore as a vital ingredient of a wise life.

Solomon saw that negotiating the way of wisdom demands diligence. It requires sticking to the task, being focused, seeing it through, faithfulness, perseverance, application and a steady willingness to do things well – all of which we can scoop up into the word diligence.

He also observes that those who are diligent get the rewards everyone wants. But those same rewards elude those who are lazy or looking for a quick profit. Let me show you what I mean.

- We all want **wealth** and Solomon observes that *"diligent hands bring wealth"* (Proverbs 10:4). That diligence is seen in our hard work, hence he observes *"All hard work brings a profit"* (Proverbs 14:23), especially when it is part of a proper long-term plan (see Proverbs 21:5).

- We all want **satisfaction** and Solomon concludes that *"the desires of the diligent are fully satisfied"* (Proverbs 13:4).

- We all want **promotion** and to get on in life, and Solomon notes that being diligent makes us skilled in what we do. Consequently he writes, *"Do you see a man skilled in his work? He will serve before kings; he will not serve before obscure men"* (Proverbs 22:29).

- Some of us want to be **in charge**, to lead the company, project, church or ministry. Solomon pinpoints that what gets us there, and keep us there, is diligence. *"Diligent hands will rule"* (Proverbs 12:24).

- And we certainly all want to be making **visible progress** in life, which again is a product of diligence as observed by Solomon and also by Paul in the New Testament who told Timothy to, *"Be diligent in these matters; give yourself wholly to them, so that everyone may see your progress"* (1 Timothy 4:15).

This shows how fundamental diligence is to our success. It truly is a "pillar" of Wisdom's House.

The enemy

However, like all good things diligence has an enemy. It lurks in our flesh, our sinful nature, and will rob us of the rewards of diligence if we allow it to. Solomon describes it wonderfully well by using the word "sluggardliness". It means being lazy, undisciplined, slow and dilatory. The sluggard can often be found trying to take the moral high ground by cleverly justifying their inaction, but wisdom sees through the sham and names it for what it is: pure laziness.

The life of the sluggard stands in stark contrast to that of the diligent. They may well desire the rewards of wealth, satisfaction, promotion, rule and progress enjoyed by the diligent, but their laziness prevents them ever getting them. In fact, Solomon observes that their lives have distinct characteristics:

- They are **poor** because *"Lazy hands make a man poor"* (Proverbs 10:4).
- And that poverty is often because they are **all talk** and no action, for *"mere talk leads only to poverty"* (Proverbs 14:23).
- They use **weak excuses** to justify not working such as, *"The sluggard says, 'There is a lion outside!' or, 'I will be murdered in the streets!'"* (Proverbs 22:13).
- As a result, the sluggard may well end up in **servile** working conditions because *"laziness ends in slave labour"* (Proverbs 12:24).
- They are **always craving**. But *"The sluggard craves and gets nothing"* (Proverbs 13:4) and *"The sluggard's craving will be the death of him, because his hands refuse to work"* (Proverbs 21:25).
- They also **chase fantasies**, but as Solomon observes, *"he who chases fantasies lacks judgment"* (Proverbs 12:11) because *"A sluggard does not plough in season; so at harvest time he looks but finds nothing"* (Proverbs 20:4). As a consequence, *"the one who chases fantasies will have his fill of poverty"* (Proverbs 21:19).
- **Self-delusion** eventually sets in because *"The sluggard is wiser in his own eyes than seven men who answer discreetly"*

(Proverbs 26:16).

What a terrible place to be in. And I'm sure, like me, you instinctively feel that the way of wisdom you are pursuing requires you to develop diligence rather than laziness. But what makes this a little more complicated is that for most of us these contrasts are not as stark as Solomon paints them. If we are honest, we are all a bit of a mixture! In some things we are diligent and in others we are a bit lazy. We quickly become diligent at the things we love doing, but tend to be more lazy about doing the things we find a chore.

The personal challenge is therefore to beat laziness particularly where the task in question is one we do not particularly relish doing. Are we diligent in saying we are sorry, in seeking forgiveness or admitting we are wrong? Are we diligent with our spiritual disciplines of reading God's Word, prayer and getting time alone with God? Are we diligent in keeping appropriate boundaries in place for our speech, behaviour and life-management?

The more you think about it, the more you will come to agree with Solomon that diligence is indeed a pillar of the house Wisdom lives in. It is a fundamental attitude, a strong pillar, a foundation stone for a wise life.

Diligence in action

Diligence is an attitude. It permeates everything about a person once it is embraced as a foundational principle to live by. But its fruit is seen in very specific actions. And the first place people tend to look for the fruit of diligence is in our work. They observe how we do our regular tasks in our day-to-day job or career and depending on what they find there, make a judgment about how diligent we are.

I am well aware we can sometimes be diligent at home with our parenting, loving our spouse and keeping our gardens tidy whilst still being lazy at work. So to just look at how someone does their job can give an imbalanced impression. But that imbalance itself needs to be diligently tackled so that we become well-rounded people of integrity; people who are diligent in every area of life not just some. Diligence must permeate all we are and do, so when people observe any single aspect of our lives its fruit is found there.

One way of ensuring that all the work you do is characterised by diligence is to ensure you have a proper understanding of what work actually is. I think people sometimes read the word "work" but hear it as "employment". But they are very different things from God's perspective. Let me explain.

- *Employment* is doing a job you are paid for. It starts and finishes at agreed times and usually has a set of specific conditions attached to it. That is why it is easy to test whether you are diligent in that environment or not.
- *Work*, however, is what we were created by God to do. It is broad and all encompassing. It is seen wherever we put productive effort into a task, whether paid for it or not.

The diligence that truly becomes a pillar of Wisdom's house – the life you are building with God's help – will be seen in all your work, not just the tasks you are paid for. That's our aim and our challenge.

Work is honourable

All work is honourable for the Christian, be it paid or unpaid, voluntary or in return for something. Working diligently is all about the way we apply ourselves, not the task itself. So we must avoid attributing more honour to certain expressions of work than others.

In modern society there is a tendency to value a person's

work purely in monetary terms, which is narrow-minded and detracts from the honourable nature of all work. We see it in the attitude that considers a menial job to be less honourable work than a professional job. Or that the work of a housewife and mother is less honourable than if she was doing a 9-5 office job. It even extends to the children who may consider the work of emptying the kitchen bin less honourable than the work of laying the table for dinner.

It is all work and should be done diligently!

I love the fact that Jesus did the work of the lowest house servant when he washed his disciples' feet. He invested a menial task with the dignity of honourable work. I'm sure he was a diligent carpenter alongside his father as they created items for everyday use as well as things of beauty, and then continued to be diligent once he was home doing the family chores for his mother. It was all honourable work. The Bible is not explicit on this, but I reckon that when Jesus was choosing his disciples he was looking for a measure of diligence in their attitude to work. He was considering: would they be willing to apply themselves to the work that was ahead? Well, not if they were sloppy fishermen, lazy tax collectors or half-hearted farmers.

It is clear that the disciples worked hard alongside Jesus and the most diligent ended up with the greatest responsibility – Peter, James and John. They led the post-Pentecost church with the same diligence they had seen in Jesus. And when other apostles emerged, like Paul, they epitomised diligence. Paul was not just a trained Jewish academic, he was also a skilled tent maker. He worked hard, whether there was money involved or not, displaying a diligence that characterised his life and its effectiveness.

All work is honourable for the Christian and our diligent application to it shapes our success or failure in life. For this reason it is important that we fully understand the place of work in God's economy.

Work is God's idea

The way some people talk about their work would lead you to think it is a burden they have to bear that is somehow linked to the curse that afflicted humanity after the Fall. But a closer reading of events before the Fall soon dispels that notion.

God himself is described as being a worker throughout the creation accounts. After the whole process we read, *"By the seventh day God had finished the work he had been doing; so on the seventh day he rested from all his work"* (Genesis 2:2).

Included in God's work of creation was the making of people "in his image". So the God who is a worker made people like himself, people who would be workers. No wonder then that he placed the man he created in an environment where he could work alongside him by caring for the rest of his creation. *"The LORD God took the man and put him in the Garden of Eden to work it and take care of it"* (Genesis 2:15). So whatever you do, don't diminish the nature of work by consigning it to a burden you have to bear and ideally want to dispose of. No, you were created to work and true fulfilment in life only comes when you do so.

Things changed after the Fall because sin poisoned everything God had created, including work. It became tougher because the heart of the worker was poisoned by sin. So work became a necessary chore for survival rather than the joyful co-working with God it was intended to be. Also, the things people worked with now resisted their attempts to care for them. The whole created order fought back; the ground threw up thorns and thistles, the animals became a threat and nature itself simply made work much harder. Through *"painful toil"* and *"by the sweat of his brow"* mankind would now work to survive (Genesis 3:17-19).

However, God never intended it to remain like that. The work of Christ on the cross started a reversal of this process. Jesus came with his message of the Kingdom of God to announce that the King was back! He defeated Satan, the prince of this world, triumphing over him through the cross (Colossians 2:15) and started a process of restoration that would ultimately result in sin, death, hell and all the consequences of man's rebellion at the Fall being removed. Its fullness will be seen in the new heaven and the new earth, which is the eternal hope and dwelling place for all who have placed their faith in Jesus, believing that he has reversed the curse of sin and assured their eternal destiny. The guarantee of that future reality is the giving of the Holy Spirit who comes to live in every believing heart (2 Corinthians 2:21), giving each of us a taste of the powers of the age to come (Hebrews 6:5).

So, as Christians, we still live in a sin poisoned world, but we bring God's Kingdom values into our world of work. As we work with God, we become agents of his Kingdom in the world, pushing back the powers of darkness and advancing the cause of Christ in the spheres we work in. We are salt, yeast and light, to name just a few of the images that describe our redemptive purpose in the workplace. We redeem work – buy it back from its curse – and do it in the way God originally intended it to be done. We work God's way, truly expressing the image of our Creator. You were created to work!

Work is God's gift

Work is such a vital part of our make up as people, that to deny it or not do it diligently keeps us trapped in the poisonous bondage of sin – somewhere none of us want to remain. So instead, we must view work God's way, and the best way to regard it is as a life-giving, energising gift.

Work is the vehicle God has given us to provide fulfilment in life. We need to work to be happy, productive and fulfilled. As such, it is God's gift to us.

Solomon drives this point home repeatedly in Ecclesiastes. It is a fascinating book to read – one of my personal favourites – because it addresses the question "What is the meaning of life?" And he weaves into his argument that right at the core of our purpose for living is the need to treat our ability to work as a gift from God. He says, *"A man can do nothing better than to… find satisfaction in his work. This, I see, is from the hand of God, for without him, who can … find enjoyment?"* (2:24). He explains that when someone can *"accept his lot and be happy in his work – this is a gift of God. He seldom reflects on the days of his life, because God keeps him occupied with gladness of heart"* (5:19). And when we get this fundamental attitude to work right, he says *"Then joy will accompany him in his work all the days of the life God has given him under the sun"* (8:15).

Working well satisfies the human soul. It injects proper pride into the tasks we are doing – whether we are paid for them or not – and gives us a genuine sense of achievement. Fulfilment in life is all about working diligently on the tasks before you today, which are God's gift to keep you occupied in purposeful activity both with him and for him.

This is why the attitude that says, "I work to get enough money so I can eventually stop working" is stupid. It violates God's purpose in creating us to be workers. Even if you retire from paid employment, you must never stop working. Over the years in my role as a pastor I have seen how an enduring work ethic has kept people alive long after they have retired from employment. The work energises them and gives each day a purpose. Whereas when people stop working after they retire from employment, they start to die and some very quickly. Obviously the nature of the work changes as we age, but its capacity to give life meaning never ceases until we move on to our new work responsibilities in heaven.

Refusing to work is, therefore, to refuse God's gift. It is choosing to live in opposition to the Creator's design and thus remain in the hopelessness and fruitlessness of being idle. No wonder the Bible teaches us to avoid at all costs both idleness and people who are lazy, especially ones who also claim to be Christians (2 Thessalonians 3:6-14).

Finally on this point, once you grasp that work is God's gift to us, you will begin to understand why unemployment is such a tragedy in our modern world. People need to be working to be happy. But before that can be addressed fully, people's basic attitude to work itself needs to be put right. Idleness is a tragedy well before the tragedy of unemployment arrives. We must be diligent first, willing to work first. Then being paid for it may well follow. In fact, it probably will because our underlying attitude is now correct.

Work makes rest enjoyable

The diligence of hard work not only injects our lives with purposeful activity, thus bringing joy to our lives, it also releases us to further happiness by way of a contrast. The contrast is with rest. Hard work releases us to enjoy our relaxation properly.

We all need rest. But rest, relaxation and leisure soon lose their appeal when they become permanent. I know a few independently wealthy people. By that I mean they do not need to work in a regular job to have enough money to live on. They have income streams, investments or inheritances which mean they could, if they so wanted, just lie on a beach and sunbathe for the rest of their lives. Sounds nice. But it isn't. I have asked them! And in my estimation they are some of the hardest working people I know. But what they also do well is relaxation. They work hard and rest well, thus maximising the energising forces of both work and rest.

Rest is always best appreciated as a contrast to hard work. As Solomon says, *"The sleep of a labourer is sweet"* (Ecclesiastes 5:12). And even God himself rested after six days of work creating the world. If he chose to rest, to sit back and enjoy the work of his hands and the rejuvenation of doing something completely different, then so should we. Again, to never rest is another way we humans violate the way God made us. We need to rest and, ideally, as a refreshing contrast to our regular hard work that we treat as God's gift to us.

Experience teaches us that resting after a period of hard work refreshes us physically, emotionally and spiritually. It was this that God had in mind when he instituted the Sabbath principle. He built into the law of Moses periods which ensured his people kept space for physical and especially spiritual rest. The Sabbath day was a day for the Lord, to keep him as their focus for he was their source.

However, today, under the New Covenant we no longer observe the Sabbath legalistically but live in a perpetual "Sabbath rest" in Christ (Hebrews 4). But we must not forget that the pattern of one day's rest in seven was instituted well before the law introduced its Sabbaths and holy days. In fact, it was even introduced before sin came and spoiled everything. For this reason alone I believe we are unwise if we do not observe God's plan for our physical, mental and emotional welfare by taking regular rest as a much-needed contrast to our hard work. Not to do so will affect our work performance and overall fulfilment in life.

A workaholic friend of mine once justified her non-stop lifestyle to me by saying that "life is for working and heaven is for resting". Well I think she will have a shock coming! I think that if God is himself a worker and that he gives us the gift of fulfilment through work, there is no reason not to expect that we will be happily busy in heaven. After all, the reward promised to the faithful steward was, *"Well done ... I will put you in charge of many things. Come and share your master's happiness!"* (Matthew 25:23). That sounds like we will be sharing productive, fulfilling activity with our master, Jesus. The big difference will be that in a sin-free world there will be no resistance to our efforts or creativity. Fulfilling work for eternity!

Our challenge this side of eternity is to redeem our work for God and balance it with appropriate periods of refreshing rest. In this way we point towards the future, to a time when we will live in eternal rest and enjoy productive work as God always intended.

Work is Godward

All this shapes the way we work. The Christian work ethic is part of our witness to the world and a practical demonstration of God's present and coming Kingdom.

That means our work ethic must essentially be Godward. By that I mean we should work as if we are working for Jesus, because he is our real boss. The Bible says, *"Whatever you do, work at it with all your heart, as working for the Lord, not for men"* (Colossians 3:23-24).

When we believe this, it changes every kind of work we do, whether it is paid or unpaid, whether raising our children or taking out the trash. Everything we work at, we work at with Jesus and for Jesus. He is our Lord, our boss and our supervisor. And with Jesus as your supervisor there is only one way to work – with all your heart!

While working, never let it be said that "your heart isn't in it". Tackle it with vigour and enthusiasm. If it is boring or repetitive, inject some challenge into it, be creative and find new ways of doing it. Be *"like slaves of Christ, doing the will of God from your heart. Serve wholeheartedly, as if you were serving the Lord, not men"* (Ephesians 6:6-7).

Work is your witness

Working as if Jesus is our boss will get us noticed. Sadly, some will think we are just trying to impress our human bosses and curry favour with them. But that must be like water off a duck's back to us. We know our true motivation and the fact is, our human bosses should find us among the best employees they have.

Paul taught the early Christians who were slaves to work for their masters as if working for Jesus, so that *"God's name and our teaching may not be slandered"* (1 Timothy 6:1) and *"so that in every way they will make the teaching about God our Saviour attractive"* (Titus 2:10). In other words, their work was their witness.

The same is true for us today. Just be sure to let good humour and friendliness prevail. Avoid "holier than thou" attitudes and if people take a dim view of your work ethic just be the best worker you can, which will ultimately *"silence the ignorant talk of foolish men"* (1 Peter 2:15).

Is the pillar in place?

Diligence is fundamental to your success. It truly is a pillar of Wisdom's House. It is seen in a godly work ethic of consistent hard work, which injects life with purpose and fulfilment. That in turn releases us to truly enjoy periods of rest and to live a balanced life rather than one of extreme idleness or busyness. Diligence gets you to your goal and allows you to enjoy each step of the journey, however hard you have to work along the way. *Wisdom Wins!* because her house is supported by the pillar of diligence. The question is, is the pillar in place?

WISDOM'S HOUSE

Thinking

A PROPER ATTITUDE TOWARDS

JESUS
'The fear of the Lord'

Chapter 8
THINKING:
The Wisdom of Concentration

It was a warm summer's evening, ideal for the final party of the LIFE Church Leadership Academy year. We were heading for a top-notch barbeque hosted by a generous family in the church who lived near Hull, about an hour's drive from our Bradford campus. So the large group of students and tutors piled into a series of cars and minibuses and off we went. An hour or so later we tumbled out of the vehicles and began to enjoy the large gardens, games and food. It was superb. Then someone observed, "Hey, the blue minibus hasn't arrived yet." I quickly checked and sure enough, it was still en route. Then the phone rang. It was a passenger on the blue bus. "Steve," an anxious voice said, "we just saw signs for Manchester. Is that right?"

As you can probably guess, it wasn't! They had been blissfully going the wrong way along the motorway for nearly an hour. Needless to say, they were very late arriving. I was incredulous. "How on earth did you manage to do that?" I asked the driver when they eventually arrived. His answer, "I just wasn't concentrating."

Of course, we shouldn't be judgmental because we have all done similar things. We have turned left when we should have gone right, driven to the office when we were supposed to be going to church, and stopped ourselves putting petrol in our diesel car at the very last moment. Phew! And some of us have actually done it. That's embarrassing. Why? Simply because we were not concentrating enough on what we were doing.

In the days when our children were younger, I sometimes dropped them off at school on my way into the office. One September day they all piled in at the last minute and off we sped. I nipped through various shortcuts and was soon approaching the Primary School when up spoke my youngest: "Dad, what are we coming down here for?" Aargh! I was taking them to the wrong school. They were all in Grammar School now and I'd been on auto-pilot.

That teatime they made great fun of me and told their Mum, "Dad just wasn't thinking." Knowing me well she replied, "Oh, he was thinking, just not about where he was going." And a life lesson followed about the difference between thinking and concentrating.

All parents know that part of growing up involves teaching a child to deliberately engage their minds in a given situation. "Concentrate!" we find ourselves saying, as we see them trying to do their homework whilst the TV is on, they are chatting to someone in the room, and also keeping half an eye on their mobile phone screen. Why do we do it? Because as parents we have learned that thinking is one thing and concentrating is another.

The fact is, we are thinking all the time, but we are not always concentrating. And that can be dangerous because the mind is an incredibly powerful part of our makeup. I'm no neuroscientist but I have studied how the human mind works enough to know it is probably the most significant life-shaping force we possess.

The mind informs and directs all we do, shaping our emotional and physical responses to a myriad of situations every single day of our life. It is the control centre for all we do. And it runs continuously at a number of levels. Even when our bodies are asleep, the mind somehow keeps everything running while we are oblivious to it. In fact, it sometimes does the same while we are awake too as I've illustrated above.

Our minds are so wonderful that they remember how we have trained them and keep many functions ticking over for us at a subconscious level. But to work at our peak, we must engage our minds on the task before us by deliberately concentrating on it. Targeted, focused thinking is always at the sharp end of our personal growth and effectiveness in life.

Concentration is focused, deliberate thinking. It is when we focus our attention on a person, problem or situation and think about it intensely. Concentration is what shapes our subconscious thought patterns and guides our deliberate choices in life. When we concentrate, we are clear, decisive and know why we are doing things. And I am here suggesting that to walk in the way of wisdom, you need not only to think, but to concentrate!

Wisdom's House is built upon a pillar of thoughtful deliberation before every action is taken. So as we explore this vital pillar of Wisdom's House, when I use the term "thinking" I will always be meaning this more focused, deliberate kind of thinking we rightly call "concentration".

The wise think

It is a hallmark of the wise that they think seriously about things. Solomon says, *"The wisdom of the prudent is to give thought to their ways"* (Proverbs 14:8). What makes them wise is that they have thought carefully about what they are doing.

Such thoughtfulness produces *"sound judgment and discretion"* which protects them from stumbling, sudden disaster or being caught in a trap (Proverbs 3:21-26). It is a prudent man who *"gives thought to his steps"* (Proverbs 14:15).

The wise think before they speak. They consider their reply before delivering it, choosing their words carefully; taking account of the person they are speaking to and those who may be listening. I cringe when I think about some of the things I have said without thinking – things that have hurt people, made me look silly or damaged relationships. Words are powerful things, as we explore elsewhere in this book, so must be thought about before being spoken.

The wise also think before they act. They think through the consequences of what they are about to do. It could be about how they will spend their time, a place they are about to go, a job they are about to take or a spending decision. The point is, all actions carry consequences and the wise think them though in advance so they are seen to have made the best choice in the circumstances.

A life characterised by deliberate thoughtfulness will be a wise one.

Thinking shapes you

Have you ever asked yourself why your life is like it is? Or why you feel the way you do? Or even why you believe the things you do? Whatever your conclusions, the way you have thought about those things has contributed to the answer.

We are a product of the way we think and the specific things we think about. That is why thinking deliberately about things is so important.

Solomon observed this principle when he wrote, *"For as a man thinks within himself, so he is"* (Proverbs 23:6-7 NASB). He sets his observation in an illustration of a stingy person who offers you one of their tasty "delicacies" to eat. They appear generous on the surface, but really they are stingy and no outer show of generosity can hide it because, "as a man thinks, so he is". Ultimately, a person's thoughts shape them and that person will eventually be seen for who they are. The way you think shapes your responses, behaviour, attitudes and actions to a very large degree. One could in fact say, "you are what you think!"

These days the life coaching and psychology books that fill the self-help section of our bookstores are full of this principle. It seems that ever since Norman Vincent Peale wrote his landmark book *The Power of Positive Thinking* in 1953, the true power of our thinking to shape our personal development has been acknowledged. But the truth is, the Bible taught it to us a long time before that. Throughout its pages we are taught that the way we think affects our behaviour either positively or negatively. And certain writers pinpoint it precisely, like Solomon does in the scripture above.

Just think about the story in the Gospels of the woman who had been ill for twelve years with a haemorrhaging problem (Matthew 9:20-22). The doctors had failed to cure her. Then she heard about Jesus and the way he healed people. Faith rose in her heart and she had a conversation with herself. It all started with a thought and, as she dwelt on it, that thought began to shape her actions. We read, *"She said to herself, 'If I only touch his cloak, I will be healed.'"* And that thought motivated her to push through the crowd, touch Jesus and receive her healing. As she thought, she became.

It works negatively too. On one occasion King David remained at the palace instead of leading his troops out to battle (2 Samuel 11:2-4). With time on his hands he strolled the palace roof and, just by chance, caught sight of a beautiful woman bathing. He liked what he saw and concentrated on the first thought he had about her, which was an adulterous, lustful one. What follows is history: he enquired about who she was, went and slept with her, she became pregnant and David ended up arranging the murder of her husband to cover his sin. What a mess! And it all started with a thought that remained unchecked. As he thought, he became.

In my experience, people who fail to concentrate on specific aspects of their life and personal development generally become something they don't want to be. The reason is simply because this principle holds good whether they consciously work with it or not. Our thinking shapes us. So if it is deliberate, conscious and well controlled thinking, we develop in line with it. But if our thinking is random, uncontrolled or simply follows what others suggest, we will become like that: a random, confused person who looks more like what others think we should be than what we really want to be.

That's how important it is to think deliberately about the right kind of things. Your thoughts are shaping you, so learning to control them is vital. And the wise know this and use it to their advantage.

Thinking sanctifies you

All we have said so far about the power of the way we think to influence our personal growth, development and decisions, has been describing a creation principle. By that I mean it applies to everyone because God made us that way. However, once a person becomes a Christian and begins to live and act in harmony with the indwelling Holy Spirit, it goes up a level.

The reason is this: we now use the same principle to help us grow spiritually as well as naturally. It becomes a powerful tool in the process of our sanctification – the process of becoming more and more like Jesus.

Paul says, *"Do not conform any longer to the pattern of this world, but be transformed by the renewing of your mind"* (Romans 12:2). The process of transformation into Christlikeness therefore involves us thinking differently. We must think of ourselves as God thinks of us, not the way we used to or as others speak about us. And as we concentrate – deliberately thinking about the things God says about us – we will start to transform into that image.

The Bible, for example, teaches that we are "dead to sin" now that we are in Christ, so we must think of ourselves that way. How? By considering ourselves *"dead to sin but alive to God in Christ Jesus"* (Romans 6:10-11). That means thinking of ourselves as dead to the old sins that crippled us before we were saved and living in line with the new nature we have in Christ. That takes concentration. But it works. As Paul said, *"You were taught, with regard to your former way of life, to put off your old self, which is being corrupted by its deceitful desires;* **to be made new in the attitude of your minds**; *and to put on the new self, created to be like God in true righteousness and holiness"* (Ephesians 4:22-24).

This whole process of sanctification – growing and changing spiritually – involves deliberate thinking and concentration.

Thinking under siege

This principle is so important that it becomes the focus of a battle we all face. Both God and Satan understand the inherent power of your thinking to transform you. God wants you to use it to become more like the person he created you to be; to be free, fulfilled and fruitful. But Satan wants to use it to lock you up, keep you small and prevent you ever bearing spiritual fruit. The resulting conflict I call "The Battle for the Mind".

The battle rages in your mind at the point where what God says about you conflicts with what Satan is saying about you. In that moment you are confronted with two conflicting thoughts that each have the capacity to change your life if you dwell on them. It is that simple and occurs many times a day as we navigate our Christian lives. It is therefore vital that we know what to do when it happens by developing a simple strategy that will win the battle every time.

Before I get to that let me clarify a couple of things. First, don't forget that this mental battle is essentially a spiritual conflict. Winning it is not simply a matter of mental gymnastics or the power of positive thinking. It is waging a spiritual warfare against Satan, who is seeking to bring confusion, doubt and fear into our minds. His aim is to lock us up and make us ineffective in our Christian living. *"Our struggle is not against flesh and blood, but against the rulers, against the authorities, against the powers of this dark world and against the spiritual forces of evil in the heavenly realms"* (Ephesians 6:12).

Secondly, for clarity, you must also understand that this battle is not a conflict between spiritual armies seeking to dominate the empty ground of your mind. Don't imagine it works like the cartoons which show an angel sitting on one of your shoulders and a devil on the other, each whispering their suggestions into your ear to think upon. No, this is not a battle for possession of your mind because your mind is already under a controlling influence. The ground of your mind is already Christ's.

The Bible teaches that because of the indwelling Holy Spirit, *"We have the mind of Christ"* (1 Corinthians 2:16). His role is to reveal truth and knowledge to us so we can choose to walk in it. He even knows the *"deep things of God"* and reveals to us *"God's wisdom"* (1 Corinthians 2:6-16). It is ours already in seed form and, as we seek it out like the diligent seeker of wisdom, it will become a reality, evidenced by the wise life we live. It is inescapable, *Wisdom Wins!*

The battle for the mind is therefore more like a siege than one for new ground because it is waged from a place of possession. It is a battle to hold the ground of your mind for Christ against any thought that tries to dislodge you. And you do that by standing firm, putting on *"The full armour of God so that you can take your stand against the devil's schemes ... so that when the day of evil comes, you may be able to stand your ground, and after you have done everything, to stand"* (Ephesians 6:11,13). In addition, you also have at your disposal the Bible, God's Word, which will inform and train your mind as you meditate on it. So there is a sense in which you already *have* the mind of Christ by virtue of the Holy Spirit in you, and alongside that you also *put it there* by deliberately reading and thinking about what God says in the Bible. It is wonderful! You can think as God thinks and therefore become like him.

But the battle still takes place. Life just happens and suddenly your mind is under siege. It may take the form of negative thoughts, memories of a past failure, pure fear or a temptation to disobey God in some way or other. The moment that happens, you are in the battle. Whether the thought is a direct response to a situation you are in or totally random, it must be defeated.

Every day we encounter both. Just recently I was driving with a friend in the car and we passed a billboard poster that said, "One out of three people in your car will die of cancer". That thought attacked both our minds and we had to deal with it by humorously saying it was "the guy in the back"! I smile as I recall it, but it is deadly serious actually. That thought, if concentrated on, could breed all manner of fear in us.

I have a friend who was very claustrophobic before becoming a Christian, but Jesus set her free and today she enjoys being able to get into cars, lifts and small spaces which she would never do before. Recently she was on the London Underground – that's how free she is – but on that particular day the train got delayed between two stations and the lights started flickering. Momentarily they went out and she was immediately in the battle for her mind. Would she pass out, scream, slip back into the bonds of fear? Well, she didn't and today she tells the story with a smile because she won the battle, but at the time she was in serious spiritual warfare.

This illustrates just how suddenly a response thought can be in our mind and plunge us into the battle. But we are also subject to random thoughts. Walking is a passion of mine. I love to walk the hills and mountains; it energises me and revives my soul. Cliffs, crags and peaks are there to be conquered and the view from the summit savoured. But as I do so, I have often found myself thinking I should jump off. Irrational, I know, but real all the same. It's a thought, a random idea. But if I concentrate on it too much I may just do it. So I have to see it for what it is, a battle for control of my mind and dismiss it from my thoughts. I haven't jumped yet and don't intend to!

I could go on with example after example. But the big question is, how do we win the battle, push back those thoughts laying siege to our mind and live free from them?

Thinking seriously

The answer lies in thinking seriously. Concentrating. Deliberately directing the mind to think about things that will benefit us and keep us in the place of victory.

This is how we wage the battle against enemy thoughts: *"We demolish arguments and every pretension that sets itself up against the knowledge of God, and we take captive every thought to make it obedient to Christ"* (2 Corinthians 10:4-5). Those thoughts are "arguing" with the mind of Christ in us and many of them are simply lies – "pretensions", trying to deceive us. So we must capture them and process them. How? By concentrating hard, thinking seriously and dealing with them resolutely.

It strikes me we are commanded by God to think very specifically at times like this. It is not a polite suggestion for us to take or leave. No, these are commands because we are in a battle and a lot is at stake. So God says, *"Set your mind on things above, not on earthly things'* (Colossians 3:2), *"Take every thought captive and **make it** obedient to Christ"* (2 Corinthians 10:5) and *"Whatever is true, whatever is noble, whatever is right, whatever is pure, whatever is lovely, whatever is admirable – if anything is excellent or praiseworthy – **think about** such things"* (Philippians 4:8). This is the language of concentration and thinking seriously.

Let me share with you how I have learned to win the battle for my mind, because it has been a major learning curve in my personal development as a Christian. I am a thinker by nature and would tend to over-think. This means that if I get a wrong thought and over-think it, I end up in a muddle. So I thought long and hard about what the Bible teaches on these things – as I would! And one day I spotted the command: *"Take captive every thought to make it obedient to Christ"* (2 Corinthians 10:5). A bit of research taught me that this verse can be translated, "Causing every thought to come under the authority of Christ". So I was supposed to take hold of a wrong thought, make it obedient to Christ's authority and then deal with it accordingly. I got that much, but then realised that to do it I needed a basis upon which to sort my thoughts out. This I eventually called my "thought filter".

I imagined my head being like the airspace above an airport

and I was the person in the control tower. An enemy plane enters my airspace and it flashes on my radar screen – much like when we suddenly become aware of a bad thought appearing in our mind. That warning initiates the "thought filter". The plane requests permission to land – that is, permission to be thought about some more. In response, I tell it to leave my airspace and if needed, send my fighter jets after it! It never lands, never gets entertained, thought about or concentrated upon. It therefore never influences my behaviour and attitudes. Job done.

The thought filter, which is central to this victory, is made up of two things: my knowledge of God's Word and my sensitivity to the Holy Spirit. So the moment the bad thought enters my mind, I take it captive and assess whether it agrees with God's Word and whether is rests easily with the Holy Spirit in me. I do it in a split second and can then process the thought further. It is this action that subjects the thought to Christ's authority.

I've come up with a simple way of remembering how to use the thought filter by linking it to three simple words:

- **Recognise:** Recognise the source of the thought by lining it up with your knowledge of God's Word and what the Spirit says to your heart. In other words, "make it obedient to Christ".

- **Refuse:** If it's a bad thought, refuse to dwell on it. Actively put the thought out of your mind. Refuse to conform to it. If necessary, speak out loud to the thought or whatever you perceive the source of the thought to be. Strongly resist this intrusion into your mind, confident that as you *"Submit yourselves to God, resist the devil and he will flee from you"* (James 4:7).

- **Replace:** Thirdly, and most importantly, replace the negative, evil, critical or impure thoughts with God's Word. Most Christians are good at the first two steps but struggle when the thought they try and push from their mind keeps reappearing as if on elastic! They key is not to leave your mind empty. Once you have recognised and refused a bad thought you *must* replace it with something greater than and opposite to it. This is where your knowledge of God's Word becomes vital. Replace it by filling your mind with all God's goodness to you.

So what does it look like in practice? Well just imagine that as you are walking along the cliff tops with me, and the thought to throw yourself off and "fly like a bird" suddenly comes into your mind…

- **Recognise**: It is from Satan, who seeks only to *"steal and kill and destroy"* (John 10:10).
- **Refuse:** Resolutely refuse it in Jesus' name. Speak out loud if necessary.
- **Replace:** Fill your mind with thoughts of God's promises to you; thoughts of the hope and future you have (Jeremiah 29:11); thoughts of your destiny and calling. Throwing yourself off the cliff soon becomes the silliest thing imaginable – you have a great life ahead! And if a tinge of fear touches your heart as the thought arrives, remind yourself of God's love and protection. Remember, *"The angel of the Lord encamps around those who fear him, and he delivers them."* (Psalm 34:7)

Or, imagine that you are in a situation at work where you are asked you to do something that you know is unrighteous. The thought comes, "I'd better do it, because if I don't, I could lose my job!"

- **Recognise:** It is from Satan, who is the deceiver and the source of all unrighteousness.
- **Refuse:** Determine not to let fear of your employer, or fear of unemployment, stop you from doing what is right.

- **Replace:** Fill your mind with thoughts of how God honours and rewards people of integrity. His word says, *"The man of integrity walks securely"* (Proverbs 10:9) and that is what you are determined to be. Be careful, too, that you don't allow the fear of your boss to snare you. Scripture warns us about this but also gives us a great promise: *"The fear of man will prove to be a snare, but whoever trusts in the Lord is kept safe"* (Proverbs 29:25). Each day walk into work saying to yourself, *"The Lord is with me; I will not be afraid. What can man do to me?"* (Psalm 118:6)

That's the thought filter in action. So just remember those three words: Recognise, Refuse, Replace and start taking control of the "airspace" of your mind for Christ. In this way you will stand in the victory of all Christ has done for you through the cross and the destiny into which he has called you.

Your mind may come under siege, but you need never lose the battle.

Thinking saves you

Concentrating on the right things saves you from so much in life. It cannot, of course, save you from your sin – only faith in the saving work of Jesus can do that. But once you are saved and secure in Christ, serious thinking saves you from all manner of attacks, diversions, random ideas and poor decisions.

But best of all, sound thinking saves you in order to do some very positive things with your life. It saves you to walk in the way of wisdom by making great choices. It keeps you conscious of heaven's values and empowers you to apply them into your daily living.

As someone who wants to walk in the way of wisdom, be sure to fully connect with "the mind of Christ" in you and allow it to inform and direct all that you concentrate on. By so doing, you ensure the pillar of sound thinking is in place as you continue to build Wisdom's House.

WISDOM'S HOUSE

Friendship

A PROPER ATTITUDE TOWARDS

JESUS
'The fear of the Lord'

Chapter 9
FRIENDSHIP:
The Wisdom of Good Company

What is a friend?

Like many of you, I have lots of social media "friends". They include a vast spectrum of people, ranging from people I see most days to ones I have met only once or twice, and a few that are complete strangers to me. So it's not true to say they are all genuine friends. Many are more like supporters or people with a shared interest. And some just love people-watching via the Internet!

I also have "work friends" that I get on well with, but I never spend time with some of them outside of the work environment. So, are they really friends? Would they not better be described as colleagues or fellow-workers?

Then there are "family friends", people who are absorbed into our extended family even though they are not related to us. They are usually there because they are friends of our parents or siblings. Some become unofficial aunts and uncles and are treated like one of the family. But are they true friends?

I have "church friends" too. People who I would never have met outside of our common faith and interest in building the same local church together. They tend to be called "spiritual family" but again, that is a broad category and in real terms they are not all true friends. Maybe a better description for some would be would be acquaintances, team members or fellow builders.

Of course, I mustn't forget the natural family: parents, grandparents, brothers, sisters, aunts, uncles, cousins, nephews, nieces and so on. Some families are small, others very large, and the blood bond means we do life together at one level or another. But does it mean we are friends? I'm sure like me you have often heard it said that, "You can't choose your family but you can choose your friends", which points up the essential difference.

Does it really matter? you may be thinking. Well my conviction is that it does – it matters a lot. That's because the people we do life with, at each and every level of relationship, have an effect on us. We are shaped by them, both consciously and subconsciously. So yes, it matters who we do life with and, more importantly, it matters which of those people we subsequently become so close to that we call them true friends. Friends influence us more than any other human relationship. That is how important they are.

A true friend is one of the most precious things in life. Friends are loyal and supportive, they tell us the truth even if it hurts and stick by us through the good and the bad times in life. Everyone needs a friend and to be a friend. Friendship is the glue of human relationships. It moves people from being mere acquaintances or task-related colleagues to someone who shares life with you at a deeper level.

Having said all that, what is a friend? For my purposes I am sticking with the Oxford English dictionary definition of *"a person with whom one has a bond of mutual affection"*.

Our English word "friend" derives from an Indo-European root meaning "to love", so the "mutual affection" part of the definition is crucial. A pure bond of friendship is the strongest relationship available to us. The parties can be drawn from any of the categories I mentioned earlier: family, work colleagues, the church family, team mates, in fact anywhere at all. There is a sense in which friendship stands apart from any task you do together, contract or covenant you have made together, or blood relationship you may have. That pure "bond of mutual affection" is very special indeed.

When true friends marry, it makes for a very strong marriage. When real friends work on a task together they tend to achieve more. Genuine friendship in the church spiritual family gives it a depth well beyond that of a collection of random people worshiping in the same location. Playing sport with friends rather than strangers is much more fun. And so we could go on. My point is that friendship enriches other relationships immensely.

Needing friends

God created people in his image (Genesis 1:26) and God is not an isolate being. He exists in the community of the Godhead – Father, Son and Holy Spirit. He is therefore intrinsically relational, which is why we are. It is also why the first thing that God said was "not good" was Adam's loneliness (Genesis 2:18). He needed companionship, someone to share life with. He needed a friend.

What God gave Adam was a wife, a pointer to the family unit that would become the essential building block of society. To be friends within the family unit is a powerful bond.

But sadly, sin poisoned that and all subsequent human relationships. Selfishness took root in the human heart. Families were broken, friends became enemies and those who once trusted one another exploited each other out of fear and a felt need for self-preservation. Finding true friendship became harder. Could anyone be trusted?

As a consequence, isolation, loneliness and a lack of true friendship now pervade our broken world. Ulterior motives are suspected when people offer friendship. Maybe they are after your money, influence or connections? Dare you take the risk? We soon learn that friends can be fickle, so we can get hurt, let down or offended. The emotional toll on us can be great, so again, we hold back and the poison of sin continues to do it destructive work.

We live in an age when the traditional nuclear family has been devastated by broken marriages, betrayal, fear and exploitation. Add to that the social mobility that modern life offers and we have a world of displaced individuals still desperately seeking friendship because God made them that way. No wonder the sit-com *Friends* was so popular. It ran ten seasons with 236 episodes between 1995-2004. Friends resonated with the innate need for friendship in us all, and if this random collection of quirky individuals could find it with each other, why not me? And so the search for friendship goes on.

As Christians we believe that God has made a way for true friendship to be experienced again. When Jesus dealt with sin on the cross, he paved the way for people not only to enjoy friendship with God, but also with each other. He redeemed true friendship. More than most, Christian's have the grace and capacity to be genuine friends to others and show the world the way. It is one of the most powerful demonstrations of the Christian life that we "love one another" (John 13:34-35). It is the way of wisdom, which is the "way of Christ". So let's explore this further and see what Wisdom has to teach us about friendship and the wisdom of keeping good company.

Circles of relationship

Think about your relational life. It is probably a series of circles. Relationships come in all shapes and sizes, but they do not all fit in the same circle. We use the circles to manage our relationships and to keep people in the appropriate relational sphere of our lives. This is a good thing, providing the right people are in the right circles. Much depends on the nature of the relationship, the expectations between you, the interests you share and the amount of time you are willing to invest into the relationship.

If your relationship circles are anything like mine you will have a circle of very close friends – probably fairly small – then a circle or two of less close friends based around shared interests of various kinds like church, sports or a cause you support. Then there will be a blood relative's circle. Maybe next is your work relationship circle, then the wider circle of general acquaintances, and then a final circle being the outer edge of your relationships where they merge into the nameless, faceless crowd you do life with. The circles intersect, a bit like the Olympic rings. People from one circle can be in another, especially when it comes to those closest to us.

This is what we see in Jesus' life. He had three close friends, Peter, James and John, of which John was his best friend. Then he had the 12 disciples who spent a lot of time with him, but not as much as his three close friends. We also read about Jesus sending out another 72 of his disciples on a mission, so he had a larger group too. Then there was his natural family and the crowd that followed him around. So Jesus had circles of relationship just like us.

From those circles he drew his true, close friends. And he made it clear that our definition of friendship – "a bond of mutual affection" – is what he had in mind with them. He said, *"I no longer call you servants, because a servant does not know his master's business. Instead, I have called you friends, for everything that I learned from my Father I have made known to you"* (John 15:12-15). Jesus shared unconditional love and his friends were the beneficiaries of it.

Solomon was equally certain about the power of friendship to enrich and shape our lives. He too acknowledged that relationships come in circles. Some he called "companions" and he observed that just because you have lots of them does not mean you will be supported because *"a man of many companions may come to ruin"* (Proverbs 18:24). So, from your companions you need to gather true friends. He also observes that the family circle is strong but may not be as strong as the bond of friendship because, *"there is a friend who sticks closer than a brother"* (Proverbs 18:24).

So from your relationship circles you will gather your close friends, the ones who will stick with you at all times and will always tell you the truth, even if it hurts because *"Wounds from a friend can be trusted"* (Proverbs 27:6). They always have your best interest at heart. In fact, *"The pleasantness of a friend springs from their heartfelt advice"* (Proverbs 27:9) which is rooted in that bond of mutual affection because *"A friend loves at all times"* (Proverbs 17:17).

Friends form us
Throughout its pages, the Bible acknowledges the immense value of friendship and the wisdom of surrounding yourself

with good company. It is for this reason that I am isolating it as a pillar of Wisdom's house. Solomon's writings in particular, urge us to make and value good friends. To build Wisdom's house, we need good, wise, supportive companions who will become true friends to us.

The underlying reason for this is that the people we choose to do life with actually shape us. Our friends form us. It happens very consciously sometimes, like when we ask for their advice, deliberately imitate their lifestyles or copy their choices. But it also happens subliminally. We are impressionable and have a tendency to adopt the attitudes, behaviours and beliefs of those we spend most time with, even when we are not concentrating on doing so.

It is a fact of life. This is why parents worry about the company their children keep. I remember when ours were entering new relational spheres, such as starting a new school, church or club activity. The big question always was "who have you made friends with?" Sometimes we heaved a sigh of relief because they were "good kids" but at other times we inwardly groaned because the child they mentioned had a certain reputation. We were very mindful of Solomon's words that, *"He who walks with the wise grows wise, but a companion of fools suffers harm"* (Proverbs 13:20). So it really mattered.

What about you? How do you select the people you do life with? Do you just take whoever reaches out to you or are you actively seeking a certain kind of person because you know they will be good for you? Solomon observed that *"The righteous choose their friends carefully"* (Proverbs 12:26) because they understand this dynamic. He points out, for example, that *"A companion of gluttons disgraces his father"* (Proverbs 28:7) because he becomes one. He later drives the point home with another example saying, *"Do not make friends with a hot-tempered person, do not associate with one easily angered, or you may learn their ways and get yourself ensnared"* (Proverbs 22:24-25).

The way of wisdom is clear: be careful who you choose for your companions because they will shape you, a principle endorsed equally strongly by Jesus and the New Testament writers: *"Do not be deceived, bad company corrupts good character"* (1 Corinthians 15:33).

It is not all bad news! So don't be living in fear that you will potentially be contaminated by the evil in the people you do life with. Remember, it flows both ways. The idea is that you, as a Spirit filled, God-loving, righteous person will have an effect on them. It is all about keeping the flow of life right and an appropriate balance in your relationships. If you didn't, then you would never ever speak to someone you considered sinful again. And that is not what God wants. The idea is that you are *"not overcome by evil, but that you overcome evil with good"* (Romans 12:21). It is about being the salt and light Jesus taught us to be, bringing his life and Kingdom values into every relationship we have. This is what keeps it safe and turns it for good. So, an awareness of this dynamic simply means that we must have the wisdom to make it work for us.

Celebrate the difference

Choosing companions carefully does not mean they all need to be like you. You may well find your friendship around similar things, which is fine. But don't fill your relationship circles with people who look, speak, think and believe exactly like you. If you do, it will soon become boring and self-indulgent.

The relationships that enrich us, spark us, and inspire us to reach higher, be better and do more are usually with people not like us in personality. Now that can make developing a friendship interesting! But the added value that flows both ways is well worth making the effort for. You will just need to keep them in the right relationship circle as you navigate through life. Solomon said it this way: *"As iron sharpens iron, so one man sharpens another"* (Proverbs 27:17). If you take two similar qualities of iron and try to sharpen one against the other, it will not work. They will actually blunt each other. To sharpen an iron sword, knife or tool it has to be rubbed against a harder quality of iron than itself. Thus, for you to be sharpened by your relationships, those people need to be different in personality, beliefs and worldview to you. This is not about one person being soft and the other hard, it is simply about being complimentary to one another. Great friends sharpen you.

In my experience, God brings people into your life for this purpose. Our job is to spot them and build a relationship for the season we are in, believing that God brought us together for mutual benefit and for his greater purpose. Back in the mid 1970s Paul Scanlon and I met. We were both newly married and committed volunteers in the church. We got on, but were very different. I was a third generation Christian, he was a first. He came from a strongly socialist working class background, whereas my family were in business and comfortably middle-class. He lived on a council estate and I lived in the suburbs. I had conservative Brethren roots, he had been saved into Pentecostalism. Needless to say, we were very different. As we emerged into church leadership together, he was the visionary apostolic leader and I was the pastor teacher. Occasionally we clashed, but more importantly, our purpose-driven friendship meant we both stayed sharp. Iron sharpened iron and for that I will be forever grateful. We are as different as chalk and cheese! But God put us together for a significant season in the growth of what is now called LIFE Church, Bradford, during which we totally reinvented it and laid the foundation for the influential church it remains today. It was a God-thing.

I often reflect on our relationship journey as I help other churches with their development today and time after time see this principle at work. Neither of us would have achieved all we did in that period if we had been surrounded by "yes men" or people just like us. The diversity in a team is one of its greatest assets. So surround yourself with true friends, but ensure they are diverse enough to truly sharpen you for the purpose God has put you on the planet for.

Friendship found
If you want to have friends, then be friendly. We do reap what we sow in life; it is that simple at one level.

What hinders us from making friends is sometimes deeply personal. It can be the fear of being rejected by the other person, the fear of knowing what to say, worrying about what will they think of us and all manner of similar issues. A level of self-confidence is therefore needed to overcome such fears, as well as a willingness to take the risk and step out.

Learning how to make friends is best learned by doing it, not from a book. So the best advice I can give you is to be friendly and put yourself into each circle of relationship you have with a big and generous heart and see what happens. God will help you as you remember that "*The righteous choose their friends carefully*" (Proverbs 12:26).

In the Bible there are many examples of friendship being outworked at a range of levels, because remember, all friendships are not equal. I don't have space to show you them all, but to help you better understand the wisdom of keeping good company, I want to draw your attention to two very special friendships. From them we can observe some of the qualities you and I must aspire to as a friend, before we can fully enjoy being the recipient of them. So there's a challenge!

In both examples the people involved love each other

deeply. They have a pure "bond of mutual affection" that bears significant fruit for them.

The first is Naomi and Ruth. They were mother and daughter-in-law, so enjoyed a family relationship, but by marriage rather than blood. Naomi was a Jew and Ruth a Moabite. So they were also of different nationalities. Life brought great grief to both ladies when their husbands died while living in Moab, many miles from Naomi's hometown of Bethlehem. She decided to return home and released her daughter-in-law from any obligation to go with her. After quite a discussion Ruth says these powerful words: *"Where you go I will go, and where you stay I will stay. Your people will be my people and your God my God. Where you die I will die, and there I will be buried. May the Lord deal with me, be it ever so severely, if even death separates you and me"* (Ruth 1:16-17).

I don't think there is a more poignant declaration of friendship than this in the Bible. It is covenantal language, not the language of a buddy, a daughter-in-law, an acquaintance or companion. This is deep mutual love and friendship.

If you follow the story it results in them returning to Bethlehem, where Ruth is something of an outsider. But her love for Naomi and commitment to fulfilling her vow of friendship resulted in her meeting the man of her dreams and marrying into the birth-line of Jesus. I believe Ruth knew her friendship with her mother-in-law was God-ordained and purposeful. I don't think she knew where it would end up, but she knew it was a significant friendship for her, so pledged herself to it. I think you and I can enjoy the same quality of covenant friendship with a few of those who God brings into our friendship circle. One should be your spouse if you are married. Others will be life-long friends who enrich the journey whatever life brings.

Consider also the friendship between David and Jonathan.

David was a country boy, raised around sheep but with latent leadership and warrior skills. Whereas Jonathan was heir to the throne of Israel, raised in the royal court and destined for kingship. They lived poles apart, yet the moment they met they "clicked". We read, *"After David had finished talking with Saul, Jonathan became one in spirit with David, and he loved him as himself … And Jonathan made a covenant with David because he loved him as himself. Jonathan took off the robe he was wearing and gave it to David, along with his tunic, and even his sword, his bow and his belt"* (1 Samuel 18:1-3).

Something special happened as David entered the relationship circle around Saul. It was a God-ordained friendship that would serve them for many years to come. In time, Saul came to hate David and wanted to kill him, which put Jonathan in a difficult position. Should he be loyal to his father or his friend?

Friendship won and throughout the story we read of Jonathan speaking well of David to his father in an effort to protect him (1 Samuel 19:4). When times got really bad, David sought his friend out so he could help him find a way forward (1 Samuel 20). It is a story of tears and affirmation of their friendship which ends with Jonathan saying, *"Go in peace, for we have sworn friendship with each other in the name of the Lord, saying, 'The Lord is witness between you and me, and between your descendants and my descendants forever'"* (v42).

Some time later, it is Jonathan who seeks out David. He reaches out to his friend at a time when he is on the run from Saul and *"helped him find strength in God"* (1 Samuel 23:16). That incident closes with more deeply meaningful words as Jonathan says, *"Don't be afraid … My father Saul will not lay a hand on you. You will be king over Israel, and I will be second to you"* (1 Samuel 23:17). This was the ultimate expression of loyalty to his friend over his father. He was willing to let his friend have the kingship and to continue serving him. No wonder the passage ends by saying *"The two of them made a covenant before the Lord"* (1 Samuel 23:18).

This was a covenant friendship seen in loyal words, personal sacrifice for the other and a life-long reaching out in support of one another whatever life threw their way. They truly modelled that *"A friend loves at all times"* (Proverbs 17:17).

Eventually Jonathan died and a grief-stricken David wrote, *"I grieve for you, Jonathan my brother; you were very dear to me. Your love for me was wonderful, more wonderful than that of women"* (2 Samuel 1:26). This was a very special friendship. I do hope you have friends like that.

Is the pillar in place?

This principle teaches us that Wisdom's House was never intended to be a self-build and that the way of wisdom was never meant to be travelled alone.

I am aware that we have treated each of the pillars covered so far very personally. It is about your personal willingness to be teachable, diligent and thoughtful along the way. Others we will go on to explore will be applied similarly. But all of them must be outworked in the context of developing good company for the journey. Some of your fellow travellers will become vital friends, God's provision for what lies ahead and people to enjoy the ride with. So choose them wisely.

Finally, think about the company you keep. Do they enrich and strengthen your ability to build Wisdom's House? If so, keep them on your build-team. If not, at the very least move them to a less impacting circle of relationship. There is no escape from this principle of life, so make it work for you as you build, staying ever conscious that *"He who walks with the wise grows wise"* (Proverbs 13:20)

WISDOM'S HOUSE

Sound Speech

A PROPER ATTITUDE TOWARDS

JESUS
'The fear of the Lord'

Chapter 10
SOUND SPEECH:
The Wisdom of a Tamed Tongue

We were half way through what was fast becoming a memorable conference. The hall was packed with delegates from every corner of the country who were eagerly devouring the top quality ministry. Throughout the day momentum had gathered and after a meal break we returned for the evening session, which was bound to be significant; you could just sense it in the atmosphere. The worship took off, God ministered to us and then we sat back, poised to hear God's Word from our respected guest speaker who had travelled to the UK from overseas just for this event.

He started well, then out of the blue he used an English swear word, oblivious to the fact that it was inappropriate. The room quietened momentarily in disbelief. *Did he really just say...?* you could hear people thinking. Then it happened again and this time the room knew they had heard it. The room cooled down considerably and he was now struggling to be received. He eventually completed his message and handed back to the pastor who, in an appropriate way explained that in his local culture the use of the swear word was acceptable, so we should forgive him his indiscretion. "Just one of those things," you might think. Sadly, not. To this day the only thing people remember from that conference is the swear word!

In the days following, a pastor who had not been present rang me. He basically said, "I won't be sending any more of my people to your conferences if that's the sort of thing you let happen." He had enquired of his people who had attended and all they had told him about was the swear word. No context, no explanation of how it had been tidied up, and no mention of the rest of the excellent, life-changing ministry they had received. If ever there was an example of how just one word can undermine and negate the power of all previous words, that was it for me.

This same danger lurks as we do our best to build Wisdom's House. The construction can be going really well, then one rash or inappropriate word can bring it tumbling down around us. Such is the power of our words. Therefore, to truly lead the wise life we desire, we must have in place the pillar of "sound speech".

Tongue power

The tongue has power, an immense amount of it. Every word we speak carries within it the potential to do good or bad. Very few of our words are neutral when we examine them closely, because they are spoken with intent and received as being meant. They flow from a context within the speaker and arrive in another context within the listener. And when that is not taken into account, the words can sometimes do more harm than the good they were intended to perform.

When you talk to someone, at least six messages can potentially come through. There is:

1. What you mean to say
2. What you actually say
3. What the other person hears
4. What the other person thinks they hear
5. What the other person says about what you said
6. What you think the other person said about what you said

Then add in the possibility that when you said it, you were in a bad mood, or just lashing out verbally, or maybe they were in a particularly vulnerable state of mind … or maybe you meant it? Welcome to the complex world of human communication. This certainly demonstrates, at the very least, the need to select the right words, deliver them clearly and take into account the way the recipient may hear them.

That's how complicated it gets! And this is also how serious it gets, because words have inherent power.

The well-known playground song, "Sticks and stones may break my bones but words will never hurt me" is untrue. We would like to think it was, but we soon learn that the words spoken to us and about us go in. They go into our heart and mind. They form pictures about us and others and become part of the inner voice that shapes us, as we discussed in our chapter about "Thinking".

The truth is that if you are told you are ugly, stupid or useless enough times, you will start to believe it. It may come via direct speech or indirectly through the media and so-called societal norms. But the words will crush you, depleting your self-image and self-confidence. Words can be killers.

However, they can also be life-givers. If you are told consistently that you are a good person, gifted in certain ways, and a uniquely special individual, you will start to believe that. Confidence will rise because of the encouragement. Self-belief will make you try harder and reach higher. You will achieve more and be happier in life as a result. Words can be life-giving energisers.

It is little wonder then, that Solomon in all his recorded wisdom devotes many of his proverbs to the power of our words. It is very clear that to him, a pillar of Wisdom's House is sound speech, which practically means taming our tongues.

His statement that *"The tongue has the power of life and death, and those who love it will eat its fruit"* (Proverbs 18:21) probably sums it up. It is that stark of a choice sometimes. So throughout his writings he contrasts the power and effects of a good, righteous or wise person's words against the power and effects of a bad, unrighteous or foolish person's words.

Here are a few examples: *"The mouth of the righteous is a fountain of life"* (Proverbs 10:11) and *"The lips of the righteous nourish many"* (10:21). He emphasises that, *"From the mouth of the righteous comes the fruit of wisdom"* (Proverbs 10:31) and that *"The tongue of the wise brings healing"* (Proverbs 12:18). More practically he says, *"Anxiety weighs down the heart, but a kind word cheers it up"* (Proverbs 12:15) and *"a person finds joy in giving an apt reply, and how good is a timely word!"* (Proverbs 15:23). One of my favourites on this theme is *"Gracious words are a honeycomb, sweet to the soul and healing to the bones"* (Proverbs 16:24). I pray you will make that your goal as I do mine.

In contrast to this he observes that *"Evildoers are trapped by their sinful talk"* (Proverbs12:13) and that *"With their mouths the godless destroy their neighbours"* (Proverbs 11:9). He teaches us that *"a harsh word stirs up anger"* (Proverbs 15:1) and that *"The words of the reckless pierce like swords"* (Proverbs 12:18). *"The mouth of the fool gushes folly"* (Proverbs 15:2) and *"a perverse tongue crushes the spirit"* (Proverbs 15:4). By way of a summary statement he says, *"The mouths of fools are their undoing, and their lips are a snare to their very lives"* (Proverbs 18:7).

That is the choice before us as we navigate the way of wisdom. Will we choose clear, positive, life-giving words, or others? Our success depends on it because our lives are filled with the fruit of our words. So I pray that you will join me in the quest to conquer one of our greatest helps or hindrances – the tongue. Taming it is vital to living the wise life we seek, so never forget that *"From the fruit of their mouth a person's stomach is filled; with the harvest of their lips they are satisfied"* (Proverbs 18:20). We want to be satisfied, so let's get a bit more practical.

One step back

Before a word is on your tongue, it has been somewhere else. Words come from the inner world of your thoughts, feelings and attitudes; the place the Bible calls your "heart". It can best be described as the motivational centre of your being. It is there that words form and then "jump" out of our mouths. Jesus pinpointed this when he taught his disciples that *"The mouth speaks what the heart is full of"* (Matthew 12:34). So if someone has a good heart, good words flow from there. But from an evil heart flow evil words. The saying, *"A fool's heart blurts out folly"* (Proverbs 12:34) crystallises this principle.

Therefore, before ever being able to tame your tongue you must first be willing to look inside and assess the condition of your heart on the matter you are talking about. Taking that one step back and prayerfully getting attitudes, thoughts and reactions right first, will ensure that the words you eventually speak will flow from a good place.

Alongside this heart assessment we also need to develop good self-control, because even a good heart can sometimes says inappropriate things, simply because we did not exercise self-control. So both need watching.

Spot the symptoms

You can spot an untamed tongue quite easily. The symptoms of what is either a poor heart condition, or simply a need to develop some self-control before speaking, are fairly obvious. The bad news is, we have all had these verbal diseases if we are honest. So before pointing the finger at others, keep your heart and attitude in check and be on your guard against these nasty symptoms:

Exaggeration

To exaggerate is to stretch the truth for effect. It is the subtle manipulation of the facts to serve a given purpose.

Sometimes it is personal. A true thing someone does is reported in a way that gives the impression it happens more regularly than it actually does. Said in anger it can come out like, "You always do that..." or "You say that every time...". Whereas in reality, it has only happened a few times.

Other times it is corporate hype. Companies, churches and clubs of all kinds have been guilty of it. You read their publicity, website or testimonials and conclude it must be the best organisation or event on the planet. Then when you go, the reality disappoints. Why did they hype it up? Simply to get you to attend. But it was counter-productive because now you are disappointed and will forever take with a pinch of salt all publicity that flows from that source.

The problem with exaggeration is that it is fundamentally lying. There is a seed of truth in it, but the impression conveyed is actually an untruth. Solomon consequently says that *"Where there are many words, transgression is unavoidable"* (Proverbs 10:9 NASB). His ultimate counsel is, *"so avoid anyone who talks too much"* (Proverbs 20:19). Good advice.

Flattery

Flattery is speech designed to use you. It is overtly manipulative and will probably include some exaggeration within it. Flattery is pitched to make you feel good, valued and indispensible. But behind the nice words is a hidden motive. What that motive is can range from the person simply wanting to make sure you attend their event, through to buttering you up so that you take on an unpleasant task they would otherwise have had to do themselves.

Once again, it is essentially lying. *"A flattering mouth works ruin"* (Proverbs 26:28) said Solomon. They are out to get you and their words are like a hunter's net: *"Those who flatter their neighbours are spreading nets for their feet"* (Proverbs 29:5). So keep your eyes and ears open for those smooth talking tricksters.

Gossip

Of all these symptoms of verbal sickness, gossip is the most prevalent and the most destructive. Yet sadly, it is probably the most common. As such it is an indictment on the state of the human heart it flows from.

Gossip is simply information you do not need to know, presented in a way that makes you want to know it. We often refer to a piece of gossip as a "juicy morsel", which comes from the following Proverb: *"The words of a gossip are like choice morsels; they go down to the inmost parts"* (18:8). The inside information on offer, or rumour they have heard, is hard to resist listening to. But we must. People who feed on gossip wreak havoc. They betray confidences (Proverbs 11:13) and separate close friends (Proverbs 16:28). They cannot be trusted. As a result, the reputation of being "a gossip" is one of the worst you can have in a community like the church.

In all this we must remember that it is not wrong to talk about other people. We do it all the time and it is fine as long as what we say is true and the way we talk about them is appropriate. If it is sound speech, it will certainly not be tainted with the symptoms of these three verbal diseases.

The tongue test

We have all been taken in by exaggeration, flattery and gossip at some point in our lives. We may even have used them. But let me keep you on the receiving end of them for now and suggest a simple test we can apply to assess whether the words being spoken to us are tainted or not.

The "tongue test' consists of three simple questions. Along comes a person you know who starts to talk about a mutual acquaintance you have in church. The information is interesting, potentially fascinating, but as a person committed to sound speech you have a reservation. So you apply the tongue test by asking yourself – and them as appropriate:

a. *Is it true?*
Don't just take what may be gossip, exaggeration or flattery at face value. Press for the truth. Sometimes you will already know that the information is tarnished and can immediately revoke it and set the record straight.

b. *Is it good?*
Think, is this edifying me? Is it helpful? Does this bless me? And how would the person we are talking about feel if they heard this? In a nutshell, is it good?

Sometimes it is important to know negative things about

people, but when gossip, flattery or exaggeration is involved, it isn't.

c. *What's it got to do with me?*
Ask yourself, why are they telling me this? What's it got to do with me? If the answer is nothing, then close the conversation down fast.

Applying this simple test will become a useful tool in your efforts to tame your tongue. It makes you stop and take control. It causes you to pause and assess why you want to hear what's coming or, if you are the speaker, why you want to say it.

When you are the speaker, it is a great discipline to be honest enough to ask yourself these questions before you utter words that are potentially exaggerated for effect, flattery to get your own way, or pointless gossip. Think: Is what I am about to say true? Are these words essentially good? And, what has this to do with the person I am telling? Train yourself to be godly in the words you speak and by so doing, tame your tongue.

The tamed tongue

A tamed tongue exercises self-control over the words it speaks and ensures they flow from a pure heart. It is proactive in dealing with flattery, exaggeration, gossip, lies, slander and any other form of verbal sin. These are the kind of actions that accompany a tamed tongue:

a. *Speak up for the truth*
Silence is usually taken to mean consent by the gossip or the flatterer. So, if their lies remain uncontested they will assume you agree with them, even if it's not the case. You must speak up.

Knowing what to say in the heat of the moment can sometimes be an issue. It is therefore good to arm yourself with a few well-prepared statements. Things like, "I'm not sure that is the case" or "No, that's not actually true." Or even "I don't think it's appropriate for us to be discussing this." And particularly for the gossip, "That has nothing to do with me, so I don't want to hear any more about it thanks!"

b. *Send them to the source*

Your pro-action will sometimes need to go a step further by insisting they go back and check their facts. It may be prudent to refer them back to their source, but if you suggest going to the actual person under discussion, it will definitely test the veracity of things. You may even have to suggest that you will go and ask them yourself. A bold move, but sometimes needed to protect all concerned.

c. *Put things right quickly*

There will be times when you are the offender. For reasons you probably can't explain, words popped out of your mouth that caused damage to someone else or trapped you in a situation you now regret being in. To use Solomon's words, you have been *"trapped by what you said, ensnared by the words of your mouth"* (Proverbs 6:2).

He goes on to urge the person so ensnared to quickly negotiate their freedom or bring things to a resolution. He says, *"So do this, my son, to free yourself, since you have fallen into your neighbour's hands: Go—to the point of exhaustion—and give your neighbour no rest! Allow no sleep to your eyes, no slumber to your eyelids. Free yourself, like a gazelle from the hand of the hunter, like a bird from the snare of the fowler"* (Proverbs 6:3-5).

This willingness to sort things out urgently, is picked up by Jesus in the New Testament. He instructs any of his followers who have committed an offence against someone else to *"Go and be reconciled to that person ... settle your differences quickly*" (Matthew 5:24-25). He later deals with the opposite situation, where you are the one offended and says, *"If your brother has sinned against you, go and show him his fault just between the two of you"* (Matthew 18:15-17). So whether you are the offender or the one offended, the responsibility remains on you to be proactive in finding a resolution.

One final thought on this process of reconciliation: don't talk to anyone else on the way. It only makes things worse if you talk to other people about the problem you are trying to resolve. You know how it goes. You said something horrid about Jenny. She is hurt and keeping away from you. So you resolve to go and see her to put things right. But on the way you bump into Mary. "Where are you going?" she asks. Now if you tell her, you are drawing another innocent person into the issue. It's tempting, I know. I mean, Mary may be able to give you some advice about how best to approach Jenny. But on the other hand, she may go and gossip about what you tell her. Or she may even be such a good friend of Jenny's that you end up with two enemies! It is always best not to tell a soul. Just walk on by and get a quiet chat with Jenny. Sorted.

d. *Face your fears*
A tamed tongue in action will mean facing up to some potential fears and overcoming them. You may fear being rejected by the person you have upset. You may even fear being punched by them! So you end up talking to yourself in an effort to justify not going through with putting things right. "He is a strong personality ... he will probably just cut me up and spit me out ... and I'm sure he will never believe I mean it when I say I'm sorry, so what's the point?"

Inner conversations like this are symptoms of fear, and the fear of man in particular. Solomon warned that the *"Fear of man will prove to be a snare, but whoever trusts in the Lord is kept safe*" (Proverbs 29:25). So face your fear and do it anyway. Free yourself from the snare and place your trust in the Lord whose command you are obeying by seeking to put things right. This strong decision shows you are taming your tongue and walking in the way of wisdom.

e. Deal with pride

The biggest potential hindrance to taming our tongue is pride. It is the first thing we have to overcome when we have spoken untruths or contributed to exaggeration or gossip. You will be having those inner conversations again, taking the moral high ground in an effort to justify what you have said. But it is always unproductive. "I'm not going to see him; he should come to me!" No. You should be proactive and go to him first and maybe you will meet half way. "I will look like such a fool." Well, you have been foolish. But you will actually look like a humble person, which is a good thing to be.

As Solomon said, *"When pride comes, then comes disgrace, but with humility comes wisdom"* (Proverbs 11:2). So choose the path of wisdom, which means humbling yourself by proactively taming your tongue.

Is the pillar in place?

Sound speech is a vital pillar of Wisdom's House. Simply put, *"The lips of the wise protect them"* (Proverbs 14:13). They protect every aspect of your life and ensure that you continue to navigate the way of wisdom with skill.

Take a few moments to think about the way you speak.

There is great power in your tongue and the words you speak have the potential to bring life or death to yourself and others. So determine to use them wisely. Take the "tongue test" and proactively tame your tongue. In the words of David say, *"I have resolved that my mouth will not sin"* (Psalm 17:3).

Sound Speech

Finally, remember that your words flow from your heart, so be willing to look within first by praying the words of Psalm 19:14:

"May these words of my mouth
and this meditation of my heart
be pleasing in your sight, Lord"
Amen.

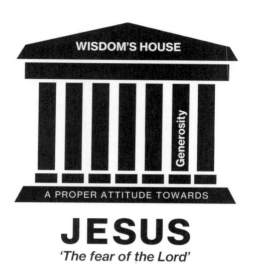

WISDOM'S HOUSE

Generosity

A PROPER ATTITUDE TOWARDS

JESUS
'The fear of the Lord'

Chapter 11
GENEROSITY:
The Wisdom of Sharing

My father died many years ago but from time to time I still find myself reflecting on his life and influence on me. It seems the older I get, the more I am becoming like him in some ways. Overall, that's no bad thing because he was a good, godly man who modelled many positive things for my siblings and me.

The reason for those reflective moments is usually me making another attempt to understand what life is really all about. I ponder on what leaving a legacy for my children and grandchildren means, where it all fits in God's great scheme of things and how I will be remembered after I've moved on to Heaven. It certainly isn't about stuff. I've got that one down, so none of that is coming with me. It is more about the essence of one's life. My Dad's values linger on even though he is no longer with me. His attitudes, demeanour and manner are what I remember more than specific experiences. His righteousness, faithfulness and loyalty to my Mum still influence me strongly. His love for God's Word and spiritual discipline continue to provoke me. And his large heart for others still challenges me, because he was a very generous man.

So I find myself influenced by my father's generosity and trying to integrate it into what I think life is all about, which may be one of the reasons I feel such an affinity with Solomon.

He too seems to have been influenced by the generosity of his father David and he also set himself the task of understanding what life was really all about. In fact, his search as recorded in Ecclesiastes and Proverbs has inspired me for years. He says, *"I applied my mind to study and to explore by wisdom all that is done under the heavens"* (Ecclesiastes 1:13) *"...I said to myself, 'Look, I have increased in wisdom more than anyone who has ruled over Jerusalem before me; I have experienced much of wisdom and knowledge.' Then I applied myself to the understanding of wisdom, and also of madness and folly"* (Ecclesiastes 2:16-17).

One of the outcomes for Solomon was the acquisition of an amazing understanding of all that God had created. He had *"wisdom and very great insight, and a breadth of understanding as measureless as the sand on the seashore"* (1 Kings 4:29) *"... He spoke three thousand proverbs and his songs numbered a thousand and five. He spoke about plant life, from the cedar of Lebanon to the hyssop that grows out of walls. He also spoke about animals and birds, reptiles and fish"* (1 Kings 4:32-33). Solomon was a walking encyclopaedia. But well beyond the factual information he gained, he managed to crystallise what life is all about better than any one else alive or dead – which is why his writings are in the Bible to help us all with the process. God gave him the ability to integrate his short human existence with the greater plan of God for eternity. He isolated what matters in life, what truly fulfils us and the values that will best support the life we are constructing. Some of those values are articulated as the seven pillars of wisdom we are exploring in this book.

Informed by experience

The other thing I appreciate about Solomon's search for the meaning of life is that he was also strongly influenced by his father. He was shaped by his upbringing and was informed in particular by his early experiences of life.

In those formative years he was being prepared by his father David for the day he would succeed him as king. His formal education would have been tailored for statesmanship and his military training for leading the army. His building construction knowledge would have set him up to oversee the construction of the Temple in particular, and the other great civil engineering projects he completed. King David shaped this process for him and ensured he was exposed to the right influences fit for a future king.

I'm sure it was the best possible preparation. But it seems that through all the formal aspects of his preparation there shone a higher, more lasting influence on the young man Solomon – the heart of his father David. Scripture describes David as being a "man after God's heart". He led Israel to its peak of power and influence and became the benchmark against which all future kings would be measured. So Solomon's real quest was to walk in the footsteps of his father David. I'm sure he asked himself many times, "what would David do in this situation?" It may even have been that question that drove him to the Lord for counsel and wisdom in the first place, just like he had seen his father do many times. And of all that David taught him, the final hand-over just before he died, must have made a massive impact on the soon-to-be-king. It was focused on what David probably regarded as Solomon's life work: the building of the Temple. And it was generous in the extreme.

"With all my resources I have provided for the temple of my God—gold for the gold work, silver for the silver, bronze for the bronze, iron for the iron and wood for the wood, as well as onyx for the settings, turquoise, stones of various colours, and all kinds of fine stone and marble—all of these in large quantities. Besides, in my devotion to the temple of my God I now give my personal treasures of gold and silver for the temple of my God, over and above everything I have provided." (1 Chronicles 29:2-3)

Solomon then would have seen that David's generosity inspired others to do the same. The leaders of the people also *"gave willingly"* and then *"the people rejoiced at the willing response of their leaders, for they had given freely and wholeheartedly"* (1 Chronicles 29:6-9).

No doubt he would have recalled the prayer of his father after this amazing show of generosity had taken place: *"I know, my God, that you test the heart and are pleased with integrity. All these things I have given willingly and with honest intent. And now I have seen with joy how willingly your people who are here have given to you"* (1 Chronicles 29:17).

What a legacy for Solomon! He had witnessed the extreme generosity of his father become contagious because people were captured by the plan and purpose of God and wanted to be involved in it. In the years that followed he turned their dream into reality, building the Temple and setting God in his rightful place at the centre of the community of his people.

Putting it all together

The knowledge gained from his search for wisdom by observing life with God's help, and the enduring influence of his father's legacy, converged to strongly establish the pillar we are exploring here. They taught Solomon that there is great wisdom in being generous. So much so, it must be a pillar of Wisdom's House.

He observed that *"A generous man will himself be blessed, for he shares his food with the poor"* (Proverbs 22:9). Generosity carries a two-fold blessing, one for the recipient and one for the giver. Hence, *"One person gives freely, yet gains even more; another withholds unduly, but comes to poverty"* (Proverbs 11:24). There is a divine principle in operation here because generosity is an expression of God's heart, which motivates *"the righteous* [to] *give without sparing"* (Proverbs 21:26). For that reason, *"those who give to the poor will lack nothing"* (Proverbs 28:27).

Summing up all he learned from his observations and his father, he finally penned, *"A generous man will prosper; he who refreshes others will himself be refreshed"* (Proverbs 11:25). That says it all.

As we then keep reading the Bible story, we bump into the wisdom of generosity time and time again. We meet kings like Hezekiah in the Old Testament who also *"did what was right in the eyes of the Lord, just as his father David had done"* (2 Chronicles 29:2). He led a revival in Israel, taking them back to being God-centred after a period of serious backsliding. Generously, he too made provision for the Temple to be restored and ensured the poor were looked after. As a result, we read at the close of his life that, *"In everything that he undertook in the service of God's temple and in obedience to the law and the commands, he sought his God and worked wholeheartedly. And so he prospered"* (2 Chronicles 31:21). The principle holds good: generous people attract God's favour.

Then as the story moves through into the New Testament, we soon discover that one of the hallmarks of the church that emerged after Pentecost was its generosity. *"All the believers were one in heart and mind. No one claimed that any of their possessions was their own, but they shared everything they had … God's grace was so powerfully at work in them all that there were no needy persons among them. For from time to time those who owned land or houses sold them, brought the money from the sales and put it at the apostles' feet, and it was distributed to anyone who had need"* (Acts 4:32-34). What a wonderful, large-hearted reputation the Jerusalem church had.

When it then came to finding someone who would open the way for the Gospel to be taken to the Gentiles, who did God look for but a generous person – someone who would instinctively share the good things he had with others. Cornelius was that person. His credential for the job were that, *"He and all his family were devout and God-fearing; he gave generously to those in need and prayed to God regularly"* (Acts 10:2). He was visited by an angel, who explained that he had come to select him for the mission because his *"prayers and gifts to the poor have come up as a memorial offering before God"* (Acts 10:4). God knew that if he entrusted the Gospel to a generous man, it would be shared freely, and the rest of story proves it to be true.

Wisdom Wins! Her house gets built because the wise are generous and willing to share. Let's now examine this pillar a little more practically.

Generosity is a heart matter

Generosity is fundamentally an attitude, not an action. Before it is seen in an act of service or the sharing of something, it is an attitude of the heart.

The truth is you can appear generous by a public display of generosity but still have a stingy heart. But God reads our hearts and rewards what he sees there rather than the outward show. He set this principle in place way back in the Old

Testament where every seventh year was a year of cancelling debts – which meant many lenders had to be generous to keep the law. Whether they would do it cheerfully was, of course, another thing. So God said this to them:

*"Do not be hard hearted or tight fisted ... Rather, be open handed and freely lend them whatever they need. Be careful not to harbour this wicked thought: 'The seventh year, the year for cancelling debts, is near,' so that you do not show ill will toward the needy among your fellow Israelites and give them nothing. They may then appeal to the Lord against you, and you will be found guilty of sin. **Give generously to them and do so without a grudging heart**; then because of this the Lord your God will bless you in all your work and in everything you put your hand to."* (Deuteronomy 15:7-10)

It all starts in the heart, much as we discovered when we explored where our words come from in the previous chapter. Everything flows from that motivational centre we call our "heart". That is why God is concerned that we become people after his heart like David was. So as you work on developing your generosity to get this pillar of Wisdom's House in place, first examine your heart.

Generosity starts with what you have

Wise parents teach their children to share while they are young. "Share those sweets with your friends," I remember telling one of my sons repeatedly. In return I got a disappointed stare and a reluctant word of agreement. Off he would go and the next thing I knew the empty bag was in the bin. Little did I know that he was being a shrewd little cookie! Rather than sharing them, he was hiding them. Only when changing the sheets on his bed some days later was the stash discovered. On questioning him about it, his defence was that "there weren't enough in the bag to share", so he kept them all!

I think that attitude is very widespread today, especially when things are financially tight or resources are being stretched. People say to themselves, "I would like to be generous and share with others but I have so little. I need to hang onto what I have to survive." It is as if we create a threshold beyond which we will then begin to be generous, but until we exceed that threshold we feel justified in keeping everything for ourselves. As a result, the blessing of being generous never flows into our lives and contributes to our continued poverty.

The other thing that can then happen is this: when we do at some point get enough to be able to share more easily – the threshold is passed – we increase the threshold! If our heart is fundamentally stingy, it will forever be coming up with ideas to justify us holding onto things rather than sharing them, and increasing the threshold is one. It all starts in the heart and must be broken there.

The revelation a stingy, begrudging heart needs to work with is that generosity starts with whatever we have, however little we think we have. Remember the story Jesus told about the rich Pharisees who made a public display of their so-called generosity? He exposed them by pointing out that a poor widow who gave just a small copper coin, actually gave more than them because it was all she had. Generosity is never related to the amount we have, it is always about our willingness to share and help others. It is a matter of the heart and begins with what we have, however small.

Paul celebrated this same quality when he was collecting an offering for the poor in the Judean church from the Gentile churches he was passing through on his travels. He was amazed by the generosity of the Macedonian church in particular. *"In the midst of a very severe trial ... their extreme poverty welled up in rich generosity. For I testify that they gave as much as they were able, and even beyond their ability. Entirely on their own, they urgently pleaded with us for the privilege of sharing in this service to the Lord's people. And they exceeded our expectations"* (2 Corinthians 8:1-5). He went on to use this wonderful, large-hearted example to provoke other churches to do the same and have their contribution ready *"as a generous gift, not as one grudgingly given"* (2 Corinthians 9:5).

Your willingness to share has nothing to do with the amount you have, it is all a matter of your heart attitude. It begins with what you have now. Are you generous hearted enough to share some of it with others? It will sometimes mean self-sacrifice. But it is never too high a price to pay for the joy of sharing with others and training your heart to be as large and generous as God's.

Generosity is life-sized

Developing a generous heart affects your whole life. Paul alludes to this after the passage quoted above about the Macedonian church. He explains that our willingness to share initiates a process of sowing and reaping. The reaping that flows back to us, whatever that looks like in practical terms, allows us to continue to be generous – and so the cycle grows. He says, *"You will be enriched in every way so that you can be generous on every occasion"* (2 Corinthians 9:11).

One of the mental barriers we have to break when it comes to understanding generosity is to stop limiting it to financial matters alone. Money is, of course, very important to us and sharing it is certainly a measure of our generosity – but a limited one.

Generosity is life-sized. Yes, it is good to be generous with our money. In fact Paul instructed the rich in particular to be *"generous and willing to share"*. But just before saying this he told those same rich people to *"be rich in good deeds"* which includes far more than giving money away (1 Timothy 6:18).

Life-sized sharing that flows from a generous heart will be seen in multiple ways:

- *Generous words* of encouragement flow from a generous heart. Earlier we noted that the church after Pentecost was very generous. Some sold land and the proceeds were shared with the poor. One of those people was a man called Joseph, a Levite from Cyprus. Have you heard of him before? I bet you have, just not by that name. He was so generous that it characterised all he did and his fellow disciples changed his name to Barnabas, which means "son of encouragement" (Acts 4:36). He was generous with his possessions and his words; that is what makes a true encourager.

So even if you have no possessions to share with others, start with your words.

- *Generously giving time* flows from the same source. The vast majority of our acts of kindness are first gifts of shared time. We all have a fixed amount of time to manage in life; there are only 24 hours in each day and we get to choose what to do with them. So, if we choose to serve someone else with some of those hours, we are sharing our time. Sometimes it involves sacrifice because we have to forego using those hours for something we personally wanted to do. But the generous, giving heart sows those hours into the life of the person being helped.

How generous are you with your time? And what is your motive for sharing it with others? Check your heart and even if you have nothing practical to be generous with, start giving some of your time away today.

- *Generously sharing knowledge and experience* is another non-financial way to positively share with others. Before I joined the church staff on a full time basis, I had a career as a Chartered Building Surveyor. That gave me knowledge and experience that from time-to-time could be very helpful to those without it. In the marketplace, that knowledge was expensive to buy, so it became one of my pleasures to generously share it with those who were less able to pay for it. To this day some friends still call me in when they have a building problem! What's more, over the years I have been the happy recipient of other people's generosity with their life experience and specialist knowledge.

This is something we can all get involved in. Sometimes we call it mentoring or discipleship, which makes it sound very grand. Whereas, if you are being friendly – as we explored in an earlier chapter – and learning to be generous with your words as we explored in the last chapter, it just becomes the overflow of a shared life. It is wonderful to have friends who love each other enough to generously enrich each other's life from their knowledge and experience.

So whatever you know, or can do, share it with someone. Go on; be generous.

- Generously sharing our **homes and possessions** is the final expression of generosity I want to highlight. We all live somewhere, and those of us fortunate enough to own or rent our own homes can sometimes treat them like our private retreat; a sanctuary from the world. That view is reinforced in my culture where we have a saying that "an Englishman's home is his castle". And castles have high walls and a moat to keep people out! How sad.

Our homes provide a wonderful opportunity to share with others. They are a "generosity tool". The proper word for this is hospitality. To be hospitable is to be welcoming; to share food, shelter, warmth and conversation with others. It is simply being generous with what you have.

This opportunity extends to everything we own. Just think about it: your garden tools, vehicles, electrical appliances, even your clothes could be shared with others. But it won't even enter your head to see them that way unless you have a big-hearted generous spirit.

So, let's stop limiting generosity to financial matters. It is a life-sized attitude that makes our lives overflow to bless others and results in us reaping the blessing of the generous. Because, *"A generous man will prosper; he who refreshes others will himself be refreshed"* (Proverbs 11:25).

The generous are like God

There are many models of generosity in Bible, as we have seen: David, Solomon, Hezekiah, Cornelius and a host of others. But the truth is that each of them was simply reflecting the nature of the God they served, just like you and I seek to do today.

Our God is a very generous God. It was he who modelled extreme generosity by giving his own son to provide the way of salvation:

*"But when the kindness and love of God our Saviour appeared, he saved us, not because of righteous things we had done, but because of his mercy. He saved us through the washing of rebirth and renewal by the Holy Spirit, whom **he poured out on us generously through Jesus Christ our Saviour,** so that, having been justified by his grace, we might become heirs having the hope of eternal life."* (Titus 3:3-7)

God was excessive in his expression of love towards us. *"See what great love the Father has lavished on us, that we should be called children of God!"* (1 John 3:1). The question now is, how will we respond? Will we accept his great generosity and keep it to ourselves? I hope not. Let's instead take determined steps to enlarge our heart of generosity by sharing what we have with others, whether it is money, knowledge, life experience, time, energy, our homes or other possessions – and by so doing, become more and more like the great God we serve.

Is the Pillar in place?
Have you learned the wisdom of sharing yet? The evidence will be seen by the extent of your generosity. Take whatever practical steps you need to take today. But remember, it all starts in your heart.

Let me close with this thought. We are pursuing wisdom. That is why you are reading this book and I hope you are beginning to understand that ultimately, *Wisdom Wins!* So ours is a noble quest. Each of the pillars we have isolated so far take us a step nearer to successfully building Wisdom's House. It involves hard word, strong decisions and determination, and all along the way we are mindful that we need God's help. And that's the good news I want to leave you with. Our great and generous God has promised this:

*"If any of you lacks wisdom, he should ask God, **who gives generously to all** without finding fault, and it will be given to him.'* (James 1:5)

God is so committed to helping you find the wisdom you seek, his large, generous, giving heart is focused on helping you acquire it as you take each positive step along the way. Lets today's step be to go and share something with someone, just like God has shared all things with you.

WISDOM'S HOUSE

Self-Control

A PROPER ATTITUDE TOWARDS

JESUS
'The fear of the Lord'

Chapter 12
SELF-CONTROL:
The Wisdom of Restraint

Walls are bad news. They block you in, hold you back and halt your progress. Walls restrict your view of the wider world and keep you small.

On this basis there are a growing number of churches in the world called "Church Without Walls". It is a statement of freedom, unlimited growth and belief in the latent potential of each individual. Walls are not welcome.

We sing about the need to remove walls too. A few years ago *Tear Down the Walls* was a very successful worship song by Hillsong United. It went:

Tear down the walls, see the world,
Is there something we have missed?

Turn from ourselves, look beyond,
There is so much more than this.

Again, making the point that the church needs to get rid of its walls and engage with the world beyond them.

People have personal walls too; walls that limit their growth and prevent them from seeing the possibilities available. So as pastors and leaders, we minister in a way that tears them down. We preach release from captivity, freedom to the slaves and liberty to the incarcerated. We want you to remove all the walls from your life and be truly free.

As damaged, insecure sinners, most of us have constructed relational walls too. They were erected to keep others out, so we didn't get hurt again. But they also trap us in isolation and loneliness. So, once again, the church minsters in a way that helps us dismantle them.

You cannot be around the modern church for long without concluding that walls are essentially bad.

Wisdom's House has walls

However, that is a very lop-sided view of walls. Walls are vital to any building and especially the "building" of your life. Walls carry the weight of the structure from the roof down to the foundations. Walls keep the elements out, enemies out and offer protection to the residents.

So, walls are not just a good idea, they are indispensible to the construction of Wisdom's House which is a picture of your life. You've got to love your walls and look after them!

In fact, God spoke prophetically to his people at a time when they were in considerable disarray and said, *"Your people will rebuild the ancient ruins and will raise up the age-old foundations; you will be called Repairer of Broken Walls, Restorer of Streets with Dwellings"* (Isaiah 58:12). God's people, who are the church today, are destined to repair walls, not tear them down.

The reason for this is that some people are in disarray, not because they have walls that are trapping and restricting them, but because their walls are broken down. They need our help as "Repairers of Broken Walls" to become structurally sound, or whole, again.

In the New Testament the Church is pictured as a building – a Temple to be more precise. It is constructed of "living stones": individual Christians who collectively constitute God's dwelling place on the earth today (1 Peter 2:5). So its walls are only ever as strong as you and me. We each carry weight, are linked to other living stones in the wall, and together we give God's House physical presence in the world. We are an interconnected, functioning community. We are God's address.

So, if our community life is a shambles, it is like a defective wall and needs repairing quickly. Sometimes it is an individual living stone that needs repairing, because we are each individually carriers of God's life (1 Corinthians 6:19). Then at other times it is the joints between the stones that need repair. And sometimes there are just great gaping holes in the wall because of our collective dysfunction.

I am therefore a fan of walls. Maybe it is the builder in me? I should say, however, that I also believe everything the "tear down the walls" lobby believe. Like all spiritual truths, they must be held in balance, and our view of walls is no exception to this rule. Some walls are bad; some are good. Our focus here is on the good ones.

Control points

For our purpose in this chapter, walls represent the positive control points of your life. They are decision points; boundaries where you say "this far and no further".

Walls demark the things you will and will not allow into your life. Think about it: there is a wall, a barrier, that lets a word out of your mouth or holds it in. There is a wall that allows a thought into your mind to be entertained or beyond which it never goes. And there is a wall that allows money to be spent or insists it is saved. Collectively those walls are your self-control.

Solomon painted a picture that encapsulated this principle precisely. He said, *"Like a city whose walls are broken down is a man who lacks self-control"* (Proverbs 25:28).

Imagine the scene: an ancient walled city with great gaping holes in its defences. Maybe they are there because of lack of maintenance or were put there by an invading enemy. The reason is not material. What matters now is that the city is vulnerable. It lacks protection and things are getting in and out that should really be kept on one side of the wall or the other. It is a disaster.

Such is the life of a person who lacks self-control. Their control points are breached, so they have little or no boundaries in place, and the result is trouble and disgrace.

I use the words "trouble and disgrace" deliberately because the Bible gives us a living example of this principle in action where they are used to describe the state of a city whose walls were broken down. Tragically, it was Jerusalem, the dwelling place of God, which is another Old Testament picture of the community where God lives which teaches us a lot about how the church should be constructed today.

Jerusalem was in ruins because Israel had rebelled against God. They had forsaken him and, as a result, their enemies, the Babylonians, had overrun the city. The crumbling walls stood there for seventy years as testament to what happens when God's people fail to control themselves in line with God's requirements.

Word eventually reached Nehemiah, who instantly grasped the gravity of the situation. This was God's address and it was in a terrible mess. The state of the city reflected not only on Israel but also on God himself. And that's why he then described the city as being *"in great trouble and disgrace"* (Nehemiah 1:3). He set about dealing with the problem, which meant rebuilding the walls. He became a true "Repairer of Broken Walls".

On arrival at Jerusalem he surveyed the walls with a small team and concluded, *"You see the **trouble** we are in: Jerusalem lies in ruins, and its gates have been burned with fire. Come, let us rebuild the wall of Jerusalem, and we will no longer be in **disgrace**"* (Nehemiah 2:17). There they are again, "trouble" and "disgrace".

Trouble and disgrace tend to characterise the lives of people who have no walls of self-control in place.

In and out
The moment we lose self-control, one of two things happens:

Things get out that should stay in:
Inside you and I are many things that should never get out; things that the wise normally deal with personally between themselves and God. I.e. all the debating, worry and fear being carefully managed within the inner world of our soul – in our mind, will and emotions.

But sometimes an *emotion* gets out that should stay in. It can look like an angry outburst with tears and fists flying. The result: trouble and disgrace. Or it may be a *word* that gets out that should never have been spoken. Off it goes doing its damage and can never be retrieved. The result: trouble and disgrace. Impulse spending does the same to us. The *money* should have stayed within the confines of our budget, but it escaped through the hole of our poor self-control in the

January sales. The result: trouble and disgrace when the rent cannot be paid. No end of bad *attitudes* can bring the same result too. Simmering racism, theological bigotry, favouritism, homophobia – you name it. If the sins of our inner world are not controlled and worked through between us and God, they may jump a hole in the wall and bring trouble and disgrace to our door.

The wall of self-control keeps them in so you can work on them. Sometimes that does include sharing them carefully with respected mentors or spiritual leaders who can be part of the answer. That helps you come to wholeness in a safe and godly environment.

Things get in that should be kept out:
The reverse is also true. Our walls of self-control keep enemies at bay.

Strong personal resolve keeps thoughts out that would otherwise take us down a path to disgraceful thinking. Well-controlled relationship boundaries protect us from getting mindlessly involved with the wrong crowd and ending up in trouble. Well-maintained ethical boundaries prevent us adopting positions that would compromise our Christian values. And so we could go on.

My point is: we must maintain the walls of our self-control. It is a crucial pillar of Wisdom's House.

So, lets get practical. You may well be reading this and thinking of areas in your life where the wall needs repairing; areas where your self-control is weak or has let you down. The big question is, therefore, how do you do it?

The answer lies in understanding how self-control works. If we don't first get our head around that, there is a good chance that when we do lose control we will cast the blame elsewhere instead of taking responsibility for things we should have handled.

Self-control is a choice

The first thing you must settle is that self-control is a choice. We all have the ability to control ourselves, it's just a question of whether we will do it or not. Therefore, to exercise no control at all is a choice, just as exercising excessive control is one too.

"But sometimes I just lose it!" people say. Or to justify an outburst they say, "The red mist just descended on me and I lost control." So it is the red mist's fault? People can annoy us to such an extent that we lose control with them – ask any parent – but is it ever right for the parent to blame the child for their lack of control? No, we know it isn't. Temptation comes our way to lie, steal, fake it, take it or break it, and control is lost. But can we ever just blame the temptation and be true to ourselves? No, however strong the temptation, however annoying the person or heavy the red mist was, our response was a choice.

Only when you accept this and start taking full responsibility for your actions and reactions can you grapple with the next issue, which is to understand the basis on which to make those choices. Or, to put it another way, where do you build the wall? Where is the line of demarcation on a given issue that should never be crossed?

To date you have made a choice to hold the line by building a wall of self-control at a certain point, or to ignore the line altogether. Why? Who told you to put the line there? Or who said it was OK to remove it? This then, is the next thing to grapple with.

Self-control is learned

The boundaries and disciplines of a healthy life are modelled for us by others. As we sometimes say, "Monkey see, monkey do". For most of us this means the influential voices in our lives: our parents, teachers and peer group. You may never actually remember thinking, "I must build the wall here; so far and no further when it comes to drinking alcohol," for example. But something or someone influenced your decision and you built a wall of self-control at a certain line to prevent you ever falling into trouble or disgrace through alcohol misuse. You learned it.

Some years ago my church began reaching children from a deprived housing estate. The levels of unemployment, violence and poverty were shocking, which had made the children very streetwise. We bussed them into our Kids Church programme and sought to integrate them with the others who came. But they stood out a mile! Their language was foul, their general attitude to authority was dismissive, and if they saw something they wanted they took it. Given the chance, they were promiscuous and exercised no control over anything much at all, or so it seemed.

These, seemingly, feral children, shocked many of our adult workers. That was until they met the parents. Home visits were a condition of the child attending the programme to ensure we were operating with proper consents, so our team went out regularly on home visits. What they found were parents as lacking in self-control as the children. Some were permanently inebriated, others high on goodness knows what, and those with whom we could have a sensible conversation seemed totally unconcerned about whether the children smoked, drank or swore. It quickly dawned on us that the children had simply adopted the values of the parents who, if they ever had walls of self-control in place had certainly let them fall into ruin. The good news is that some of those children found Jesus and have now broken the generational cycle they were raised in.

I couldn't help comparing those experiences with my own upbringing. As a very young child my parents were deeply involved with the Plymouth Brethren movement, who had lots of walls. They veered towards being rather austere and legalistic about anything considered "worldly". I was, for example, not allowed to play out with my non-Christian friends on a Sunday and certainly could not shop – not even for an ice cream in summer. We had no TV in the house and I wasn't allowed to go to the cinema. Pop music and dancing were similarly associated with "worldliness" and banned in our effort to maintain values appropriate for godly people. It was all a matter of ensuring the walls of self-control were maintained along the lines of that particular belief system.

Both extremes illustrate my point: self-control is to some extent learned from the influential people we do life with. At some point we all need to stop and dare to ask, "who says the walls of self-control should be where we have built them? And why?" It is good to know where you have learned things from; it helps you understand yourself.

Having said that, most Christian people will be seeking to exercise their self-control in accordance with God's pattern for living rather than just following any human influence. Instinctively they know that is how it should be. After all, God made them and knows what is best for them. So the aim becomes to learn God's ways and establish their walls of self-control on the boundary lines he recommends.

This is a sound process because walls are built on a foundation and Jesus is the ultimate one: *"For no one can lay any foundation other than the one already laid, which is Jesus Christ"* (1 Corinthians 3:11). So we aim to learn self-control from Jesus. Practically that means reading the Bible, which teaches us who God is and what he thinks about things. It also reveals Jesus to us and urges us to imitate him.

We also learn self-control from Christ's body, the church. Other Christ-followers with more experience than us are instructed to teach us how to live; and learning where the self-control boundaries lie forms part of it. It is, to some extent, generational. Just note how the following instruction flows down from age to youth with an emphasis on issues that require self-control:

*"Teach the **older men** to be temperate, worthy of respect and sound in faith, in love and in endurance. Likewise, teach the **older women** to be reverent in the way they live, not to be slanderers or addicted to much wine, but to teach what is good. Then they can train the **younger women** to love their husbands and children, to be self-controlled and pure, to be busy at home, to be kind, and to be subject to their husbands, so that no one will malign the word of God. Similarly, encourage the **young men** to be self-controlled."* (Titus 2:2-6)

The church community is therefore one of the best places to learn how to erect your walls of self-control in the best possible position.

So, self-control is a *choice*. That choice demands we *learn* from God, and each other, where the walls of self-control should be built as we navigate the Christian life.

But there is one other vital component to include in your developing understanding of how self-control works:

Self-control is latent

Self-control is always possible for the Christian because it is not just learned, it is latent.

Latent means something exists but is not yet developed, like a talent or gift that you discover late in life. It was always there but remained undeveloped until one day you tried something and discovered you were good at it. For me it was writing. I was never that good at English language at school, but well into my ministry life one of my spiritual fathers said, "Steve, you are a very good writer you know; maybe one day you will write a book." I was initially dismissive, even though I had come to enjoy word craft. He persisted and eventually his encouragement led to me writing my first Abundant Life Skills book, *Battle For The Mind*, first published in 1985 and still going strong. I am still amazed how many people can be helped through the written word and I still love doing it.

Scripture teaches that latent within each of us are a number of gifts and abilities. They are there by virtue of the indwelling Holy Spirit and one of them is self-control. *"For God did not give us a spirit of timidity, but a spirit of power, of love and of self-discipline"* (2 Timothy 1:7). You have it! Another way to think of it is as fruit of the Holy Spirit: he is the root and self-control is the fruit we enjoy for keeping him central in our lives and living in harmony with him. *"The fruit of the Spirit is ... self-control"* (Galatians 5:22-23). It is fruit you can bear because its source lives within you.

The Holy Spirit empowers us to live a self-controlled life. As we develop our relationship with God he teaches us his ways. We learn and he gives us the strength to harness our free will, so we make great choices and keep the walls of our self-control in good condition. What is learned and latent becomes a reality.

This is just another wonderful expression of God's grace towards us. His undeserved favour which *"teaches us to say 'No' to ungodliness and worldly passions, and to live self-controlled, upright and godly lives"* (Titus 2:12).

So, the closer you walk with Jesus, the more you will learn self-control and the more you will release the Spirit of self-control that is latent within you.

Self-control looks after you

With this understanding of how self-control works in place you can get busy repairing any holes in your walls. Before long you will love those walls because they will be doing what walls do – protecting you. Self-control looks after you. It keeps you safe, secure and confident.

Taking a step back and bringing the six pillars we have already explored into view alongside this one, it quickly becomes apparent that building Wisdom's House – a wise life – involves them all working together. In particular, they each rely to some extent on the strength they get from being alongside this pillar of self-control. Let me show you how:

Pillar 1 – TEACHABILITY

Being a teachable, learner for life requires great self-control. At times you will be choosing to study rather than play, or choosing to retrain over staying in the same old job. It is self-control that will ensure you see the course through to the end. Much of the learning you do will be in the flow of doing life with God, which demands you stay in close relationship with him, which means keeping sin at bay by controlling yourself.

Pillar 2 – DILIGENCE

The wisdom of being willing to work hard demands application, focus and determination. Self-control ensures you defeat apathy and laziness. It prevents you ever settling for less than God's best. When working alone, the temptation to slacken off will come and try to undermine the wall of self-control that keeps you working just as hard when being watched as when you are alone.

Pillar 3 – THINKING

If the enemy can gain access to your mind, you will end up in "trouble and disgrace" because, *as a man thinks within himself, so he is*" (Proverbs 23:7). But the self-controlled mind will *"Take every thought captive"* (2 Corinthians 5:10) every time a bad one enters your head. It will help you to recognise, refuse and replace them with good, godly thoughts that keep you in a process of daily transformation into Christlikeness. Self-control obeys the command to *"Set your mind on things above"* (Colossians 3:2). What a great protection.

Pillar 4 – FRIENDSHIP
Self-control will help you manage your complex matrix of relationships. Where poor relationships are influencing you negatively, it will give you strength and a basis on which to extract yourself from them with wisdom and tact. It will also provoke you to keep doing good to those special friends who are vital to your well-being.

Pillar 5 – SOUND SPEECH
Do you talk too much, speak rashly, flatter, exaggerate or gossip? Your wall of self-control can stop it. It will help you to ensure that a word only gets through it if it is good, helpful and life giving. It will help you live in line with God's instruction to *"be quick to listen and slow to speak"* (James 1:19). Get the wall in the right place and it will look after you. Before long you will be known for your wise words, for speaking at the right time, and rarely be heard "putting your foot in it" because *"The one who has knowledge uses words with restraint"* (Proverbs 17:27).

Pillar 6 – GENEROSITY
When out of control, money is a great destroyer leading to the trouble and disgrace of debt, worry, sickness, envy, greed, theft, deceit and more. You must control it or it will control you, which you do by having a budget, being righteous with it and sharing it. So get the wall in place. But beyond money, any decision to be generous and share requires self-control. The over-generous can soon become worn out with doing good, and that is just as much a product of a lack of self-control as is found in the stingy soul. Today, take control of your time,

money, skills and energy, sharing generously as God leads you and the promise that *"he who refreshes others will himself be refreshed"* will be yours (Proverbs 11:25).

The stability of Wisdom's House relies on having all these pillars in place, especially the one of self-control. We live in a world where standards of morality are low; toleration and freedom of expression are the order of the day. But the God we love and serve – the one who made us – did not create us to be amoral. He made us to reflect his image and express his healthy values on matters of morality and conduct. Only as we do so does life become a wholesome, happy and fulfilling experience. That is why Christ-followers must build their walls of self-control on Jesus, the true foundation, and along the moral and behavioural lines he has established for human conduct.

Within the walls of godly self-control there is freedom from trouble and disgrace. We are protected from all that seeks to enter our space with destruction in mind. And the peace, dignity and deep sense of security we have through being in Christ is never lost.

Is the Pillar in place?

I hope so.

This one is absolutely indispensible if you are to build Wisdom's House with skill. But more than that, only as your house is kept in order are you then able to outwork your God-given mandate as a *"Repairer of Broken Walls"* (Isaiah 58:12). For just as you learned self-control from others, people are now looking to you for skill and wisdom to repair their corporate and personal walls of self-control. As you do your part, God will do his because remember, he is the latent power within every one of us.

So, before you go charging off to make your mark on the

world and be the hero, take a moment to reflect on the condition of this important pillar, remembering the words of our wise friend Solomon: *"Better a patient person than a warrior, one with **self-control** than one who takes a city"* (Proverbs 16:32).

Chapter 13
The Fool's House

There it is. *"Wisdom has built her house; she has set up its seven pillars"* (Proverbs 9:1) and we have explored what I think those seven pillars constitute. They are seven indispensible qualities for the building of a wise life on the foundation of a healthy relationship with God. Together they ensure *Wisdom Wins!*

We have spoken a lot about Solomon along the way. I'm sure like me, you noticed that a feature of his writing about the process of living a wise life is sharpened by placing his observations in contrast. The positive is set alongside the negative to make it shine all the brighter. So we grasp the wonder of Wisdom because it is contrasted with the error of Folly.

This helpful literary device is one I want to use in this final chapter. So take your "I want to live a wise life" hat off for a moment and put on one that says, "I want to live a foolish life."

Imagine that you have picked up a guide book on living the life of a fool because you despise wisdom and genuinely want to enjoy a hedonistic lifestyle. What first impresses you as you browse through the introduction is that the author does not seem to believe there is a God. Perfect. You are in good company, because *"The fool says in his heart there is no God"* (Psalm 14:1) – and you believe that absolutely.

You soon grasp the book's essential concept. The life you are building is likened to building a house. The author is saying that once the foundation of "not believing in God" is in place, you can successfully build the Fool's House by embracing a number of life-shaping principles. One might call them the "Seven Features of Folly". You feel sure there are probably more than seven, but why look for more if seven does the job?

So you snuggle down into your lazy-boy sofa, excited to learn more about the wisdom of folly, which reads something like this:

Thanks for picking up this short book about the virtue of Folly!

I've kept it short because if, like me, you are a serious seeker of Folly, you won't be much of a reader. But stick with me and you will soon be amazed how quick and easy it is to become an expert in all things foolish. All you need are seven simple principles:

1. Don't Think

First, to be unwise, you must cease from all productive mental activity. It is very important to protect your mind from what our wise friends like to call "solid food". Instead, look for mental "junk food".

The best things to think about are the shallow and the trivial.

In fact, anything that does not really require you to use your mind. It's pretty easy to find these days, what with the Internet and digital TV there is a panacea of mindless trash. And the best thing is, you don't have to look very hard, it's lying around all over the place!

Just one word of caution though, about Soap Operas in particular. Generally they are mindless enough to be a good watch but sometimes, under the guise of mindless entertainment, they slip in a "moral" for people to think about. That's naughty and can easily ruin it for you. So look out for those moralising snippets in amongst your TV trash and hit the fast forward button.

If you are going to develop the Fool's skill of not thinking, you are first going to have to avoid anything that would lead to it. So watch what you do and where you go. A few bits of practical advice from my journey into folly may help you: playing sport is in, but going to church is out. Movies are fine, but museums are not. Celebrities are in, documentaries are out. Bin the broad sheets, buy the tabloids. Forget the financial pages, focus on the funnies. But still, take care, some cartoonists are sneakily trying to make you think.

There are, of course, times in life when thinking seems like the thing we should be doing. You know, in times of tragedy, births, deaths and the like. But don't be deceived, they are all designed to hijack the empty-headed fool into life and force them into inner contemplation. Happily, however, at times like these the unthinking soul has several escape routes. We have the gift of alcohol, which is primarily designed for the quick get-away from thinking. Getting "blotto" with your mates is guaranteed to paralyse the beginnings of any serious thought. Then we have the opportunity to party, which always dulls the mind as long as the music, booze and drugs are flowing freely. Another great escape is to get really interested in something that doesn't talk back to you. Things like cars, cooking, football or fishing.

These are all helpful for distracting us from reflecting on anything serious, should we be tempted to do so. They will have done their job well if thinking about them keeps us from thinking about the so-called "main thing", whatever that's supposed to mean.

2. Never be serious

Being a great fool and being serious are just not compatible. To *be* a fool you have to *play* the fool, it is that simple.

Don't slip into the error of expressing a "measured judgement" about anything at all. I mean, that would imply you'd been thinking, and we've already established that is out of bounds!

So, our attitude to life must be to make light of everything, just like they did in the olden days. In ancient times, when kings felt the pressure of "having to be serious" about things closing in, they called for the court Jester. What a great system. And we can do the same today. Fick those channels. How awesome is digital TV! There's every inane sitcom and comedian you could ever want on tap.

So, avoid that intense look and never subject yourself to the furrows of a concentrating forehead, because life's a party!

3. Do as you feel

This particular pillar of Folly's House had excellent air play in the 1960s when "If it feels good, do it" was the watchword. And it has not lost its importance for us in our pursuit of all things foolish.

If you are to stay within the confines of true Folly, you must base all your decisions on the emotion you feel in the moment: if it feels good, just do it! So, if you want to spend, spend; to try that drug, go for it; to sleep with someone, bring it on; to take a risk, go for it.

The wonder of living by your feelings is that you never have to endure anything. Things like persistence, endurance, commitment and resistance need never be experienced if you get this one right. It's brilliant. Doing as you feel just allows us to cop out and run away – how cool is that!

Always choose the path of least resistance, then the road will always be downhill. It feels so good to have the wind rushing through your hair, just as it does through your empty head. The important thing is to experience life – to *feel* it – not to think about it, get serious about it, or go against its flow.

The subjective must always be the measure of what is right and wrong for us as fools. So, for example, if I don't feel I love you, I must leave you, for feelings are my guide and my governor. Without obeying them, I would soon stray from the road of folly.

4. Make stupid friends

Note this, because it's very important to your quest for foolishness. We become like those we do life with. So we must take this principle and make it work for us by surrounding ourselves with fools.

It's a fact: two funny people are funnier together. Think: Sooty and Sweep, Morecambe and Wise, Cannon and Ball, Max and Paddy. Simply put, stupidity is amplified by having two silly people together.

So, if you are only slightly foolish, the best way to become fully qualified is to get to know the experts by finding some really stupid friends. Their prowess will soon rub off on you. And if you do tire of their company, don't worry, there are many more around. You can work your way through an amazing array of nincompoops ranging from the sports nut, the health-food fiend, the religious weirdo, through to tree huggers, binge drinkers, tea-leaf readers and placard wavers.

The quantity of foolish friends is endless and the quality doesn't really matter. So go make some stupid friends.

5. Stick to your guns

Stubbornness is a must for those who wish to escape the clutches of wisdom for the long-term. Your will must be exercised in such a way that, however crazy the path, nothing will detract or deviate you from the course. Such stubbornness is highly prized in the company of fools.

It feels so good to hear your fellow-fools saying, "You showed them ... they couldn't convince you!" as they pat you on the back for sticking to your guns. What a wonderful state to be in. How secure and confident it makes you feel to have the ability to believe in your own opinions, regardless of their accuracy.

But be warned: such strength of will requires great determination. Even the most hardened of fools can begin to melt when faced with the intense heat of evidence to the contrary. Every fool must, therefore, have a heavy dose of that much-prized virtue of the dimwits: pride.

Only the proud and the arrogant will survive. So put your head up and refuse to let the idea that "you could be wrong" ever enter your mind.

6. Develop a short memory

Developing as a fool requires us to keep a short memory. The basic idea is to hold our position by always forgetting what has happened before, which is quite a skill.

Basically, you must learn nothing from experience. As fools we believe that everything is arbitrary and without pattern. So there is no value whatsoever in knowing what happened to others who have taken similar stances to us. We therefore only hold onto things that support our view and erase all else. Only this moment is important; the future and the past are just vanishing mists.

So the competent fool must develop two things: First, a high form of selective amnesia. After all, why trawl up the past? It's only today that matters. And Second, we must never admit error.

Thus, selective memory loss and revision of the facts are the order of the day for most fools. By this they protect their folly.

7. Criticise continually

Lastly, in order to stay proficient in the art of Folly, the guns of sarcasm, cynicism and cultivated ignorance must be turned outwards. The ability to criticise that which we know absolutely nothing about must rank as one of our greatest abilities. Criticising allows us, the fools in this world, to feel a part of the action whilst merely spectating. Now to me, that's wisdom not folly!

All you have to do is let your mouth work overtime and a wonderful sense of false-importance and significance will sustain you.

This particular pillar of Folly's House will demand that you use more mental energy than when developing the others, and actually proves that to be a fool, you actually have to be quite smart. You see, it is not the ability of your brain that is the source of stupidity, but the use to which it is put. So use it for the right things. Celebrate your prejudices rather than analysing them. Great performances can be put down rather than learned from. And use your creativity learning how *not* to do things, so as to escape responsibility and shirk tough assignments. That's mental energy well spent.

So there you have it, the seven pillars of Folly's House. I'm sure there are more, but I can't be bothered looking for them right now. So off you go and do your very best. Remember,

- Don't think
- Never be serious
- Do as you feel
- Make stupid friends
- Stick to your guns
- Develop a short memory
- Criticise continually

It's not that hard, otherwise I wouldn't be suggesting it, and I can assure you from experience that their continual practice will help foolishness to flourish in your life and prevent wisdom from ever darkening your door.

Happy Jesting!

WISDOM'S HOUSE

Teachability · Diligence · Thinking · Friendship · Sound Speech · Generosity · Self-Control

A PROPER ATTITUDE TOWARDS

JESUS
'The fear of the Lord'

Epilogue

It is still happening. People are still asking me for "a bit of wisdom" and I'm sure people are asking you too.

My hope is that after exploring the nature of wisdom with me in this book, you are now better equipped to point them in the right direction. In particular, I pray you will more consciously point people to Jesus, *"In whom are hidden all the treasures of wisdom and knowledge"* (Colossians 2:2-3).

The way of Christ truly is the "Way of Wisdom". And to build Wisdom's House is to build a life in which Jesus would be pleased to dwell.

So, I close with one of his insightful stories about a wise man. Jesus said,

"Therefore everyone who hears these words of mine and puts them into practice is like a wise man who built his house on the rock. The rain came down, the streams rose, and the winds blew and beat against that house; yet it did not fall, because it had its foundation on the rock. But everyone who hears these words of mine and does not put them into practice is like a foolish man who built his house on sand. The rain came down, the streams rose, and the winds blew and beat against that house, and it fell with a great crash." (Matthew 7:24-27)

This story sums up so much of what we have explored together in this book: Jesus is the Rock on which we build the "house" of our lives. He is the one true foundation. Wisdom begins there, based solidly on the firm foundation of a healthy, reverential respect for who God is: *"The fear of the Lord is the beginning of Wisdom"* (Proverbs 1:9).

Wisdom's seven pillars then rise up from the foundation of Jesus. They are each connected to him in that they are fundamental Christian truths. They are found in the whole of Scripture and are timeless expressions of God's will for us as his people.

As we hear these words from God and "put them into practice", Wisdom's House is built. Our lives become characterised by the *"wisdom from heaven"* (James 3:17) rather than the wisdom of this world.

Wisdom's House will withstand the storm and endure the hurricane, drought or famine. It will not fall. In sad contrast, Folly's House crashes down when the storm comes because of its poor foundation and insubstantial pillars.

I am left in no doubt that *Wisdom Wins!* It wins the argument, the war, the battle and ultimately the prize. So, it becomes of paramount importance to *"Get Wisdom"* (Proverbs 4:7).

So, my closing prayer is that you will choose wisdom and seek it with all your heart:

Epilogue

"Then you will understand what is right and just and fair—every good path. For wisdom will enter your heart, and knowledge will be pleasant to your soul. Discretion will protect you, and understanding will guard you" (Proverbs 2:9-12).

Appendix

Here is a more comprehensive list of statements by or about the person Wisdom in Proverbs, which point us to Jesus:

WISDOM	CHRIST
Pr. 8:23: I was appointed from eternity, from the beginning, before the world began.	Jn. 1:1-3: In the beginning was the Word...
Pr. 8:27: I was there when he set the heavens in place, when he marked out the horizon on the face of the deep.	...And the word was with God, and the word was God. Through him all things were made; without him nothing was made.
Pr. 8:30: Then I was the craftsman at his side.	Heb. 1:2: His son…. Through whom he made the universe
Pr. 8:22: The Lord brought me forth as the first of his works, before his deeds of old.	Col. 1:17: He is before all things, and in him all things hold together.
Pr. 8:30: I was filled with delight day after day, rejoicing always in his presence.	Lk. 3:22: You are my son, whom I love; with you I am well pleased Jn. 17:24: You loved me before the creation of the world
Pr. 8:14: Counsel and sound judgment are mine; I have understanding and power.	1 Cor. 1:30: Christ Jesus who has become for us wisdom fro God
Pr. 2:4: If you look for it as for silver and search for it as for hidden treasure.	Col. 2:3: In whom are hidden all the treasure of wisdom and knowledge.
Pr. 1:20,23: Wisdom calls aloud in the street… if you had responded to my rebuke.	Mt. 18:3: And he said 'I tell you the truth. Unless you change … You never enter the kingdom of heaven.'
Pr. 1:33: But whoever listen to me will live in safety and be ease, without fear of harm.	Mt. 11:28: Come to me all you who are weary and burdened, and I will give you rest.
Pr. 8:1,4: Does not wisdom call out? I raise my voice to all mankind.	Jn. 7:37: Jesus stood and said in a loud voice, 'If anyone is thirsty, let him come to me and drink.'
Pr. 9:5: Come, eat my food and drink the wine I have mixed.	Jn. 6:35: He who comes to me will never go hungry and he who believes in me will never be thirsty.
Pr. 8:17: I love those who love me, and those who seek me find me	Gal. 2:20: The Son of God, who loved me Mt. 7:7: Seek and you will find
Pr. 8:35: For whoever finds me finds life and receives favour from the Lord	Jn. 6:47: I tell you the truth, he who believes has everlasting life.
Pr. 8:6: Listen, for I have worthy things to say, I open my lips to speak what is right.	Lk. 4:22: All … were amazed at the gracious words that cam from his lips.